Working at Home While the Kids Are There, Too

By
Loriann Hoff Oberlin

CAREER PRESS
3 Tice Road, P.O. Box 687
Franklin Lakes, NJ 07417
1-800-CAREER-1
201-848-0310 (NJ and outside U.S.)
Fax: 201-848-1727

WORKING AT HOME WHILE THE KIDS ARE THERE, TOO
ISBN 1-56414-305-8, $12.99
Cover design by Foster & Foster
Printed in the U.S.A. by Book-mart Press

To order this title by mail, please include price as noted above, $2.50 handling per order, and $1.50 for each book ordered. Send to: Career Press, Inc., 3 Tice Road, P.O. Box 687, Franklin Lakes, NJ 07417. Or call toll-free 1-800-CAREER-1 (NJ and Canada: 201-848-0310) to order using VISA or MasterCard, or for further information on books from Career Press.

Excerpted from "What Kind of Faith Do I Want to Have?" by Rev. Richard R. Ollinger. Reprinted with permission. © 1997 by Richard R. Ollinger.

Portions of *Mister Rogers Talks with Parents* by Fred Rogers and Barry Head. Reprinted with permission. © 1983, Family Communications, Inc.

Library of Congress Cataloging-in-Publication Data

Hoff Oberlin, Loriann, 1961
    Working at home while the kids are there, too / by Loriann
Hoff Oberlin.
        p.   cm.
    Includes index.
    ISBN 1-56414-305-8
    1. Home-based business--Management. 2. Self-employed.
3.   Work and family. I. Title.
HD62.38.H643   1997
658'.041--dc21   97-17757
                                                        CIP

Dedication

To my sons, Andy and Alex.
Without them I could not have written this book.

Acknowledgments

This is the book I've always wanted to write! But without the advice, guidance, and hard work of many others, the idea would have remained in a drawer, not on a shelf!

Thanks to Jeff and Deborah Herman, my literary agents, for believing in the project and successfully marketing it, and to the folks at Career Press for recognizing its potential. In particular, Ellen Scher, Jane A. Brody, and Betsy Sheldon helped shape the manuscript and presentation of the book you're reading.

Friends, fellow home-based workers, and other authors have also contributed their wisdom where work and parenting are concerned—among them Carol Anderson, Ph.D., David Bartley, Janet Bodnar, Jennifer Boerio, Alice Bredin, Arlene Eisenberg, Cindy Etling, Donna Israel, Nanette Kirsch, Vicki Lansky, Jan Larkey, Dr. Kevin Leman, Gail Martin, Tova Navarra, Dick Ollinger, Pam Price, Fred Rogers, Hedda Sharapan, Murray Thompson, Ph.D., and Jodi Wood. David Kearney contributed his Web site development and promotion skills.

To Nancy Thompson and the staff of Mother's Day Out, I'm very grateful for your wonderful care and for the much needed support that the program gave my family.

Special thanks goes to Andy and Alex Oberlin, my two favorite guys in the world. All I ever need to do is look at them, and I know why I work from home. They make it all worthwhile!

Contents

Introduction—The best of both worlds   **9**

Chapter 1—Choosing a home-based career   **13**
Is telecommuting for you? • What's out there? • Become a trend spotter • The bottom line • How to assess your skills • What to do when you're downsized • What business should I pursue? A dozen determining factors • Fostering family support • Avoiding work-at-home scams • Providing in-home childcare • Money-making ideas • Resources

Chapter 2—Launching your business   **29**
Business plans that win you the work • Naming your business • Business cards and stationery • Setting your hours • Smart financial strategies • Tax implications of home businesses • Zoning, permits, and other important considerations • Getting organized • Working with your spouse • How to switch mental gears • Maintaining a positive mental attitude • Resources

Chapter 3—Carving out a workspace   **47**
Location, location, location • Six ways to clear clutter • How to convert almost any space to a workplace • Still no space...now what? • Finding the right furniture • Childproofing your office • Selling outside your home • Do you *really* need a computer? • Shopping for computer equipment • Printing prerequisites • Seeking technical assistance • Keeping your computer clean • Selecting a cellular phone • Saving the earth from your own office • Resources

Chapter 4—Starting small, building big   **65**
Loriann's top 10 home-business mistakes • Stay small for the short-term • Create a "board of directors" • Making a small business look larger • Networking your way to more business • Hiring extra help in your home office • Raising the cash you need • Financial records • Insurance • Seeking legal solutions • Collecting from slow payers • Resources

Chapter 5—Promoting your business   **77**
Word of mouth: still the best form of advertising • Powerful writing rules • How to write a news release • Making friends with the media • The basics of advertising • Direct mail • Selling yourself with newsletters • 12 ways to toot your horn • Targeting television talk shows • The benefits of videos and infomercials • Selling yourself on the Internet • Calming sales-call phobia • Resources

Chapter 6—Time- and money-saving tactics   95

Dealing with distractions • Keeping up with housework • Chores children can do • "Someone help me, please!" • Meal-planning made easy • Simplifying holiday hassles • Time-saving strategies • Mastering money without becoming miserly • Outfitting kids for less • Business trip packing list • Conference costs and concerns • Maximizing technology and minimizing cost • Top 10 ways to save on office supplies • Saving on paper and printing • More ways to stretch the business dollar • Finding affordable health insurance • Building your savings • Resources

Chapter 7—Choosing childcare that's right for you   117

Hiring in-home caregivers • The *au pair* alternative • Selecting group care • Mister Rogers on choosing childcare • Special-needs children • Childcare when your child is ill • Easing separation anxiety • How to find baby sitters • Baby-sitter training • Top 10 list to leave any caregiver • Picking a preschool • Single parent relief • Out-of-town childcare • Are childcare expenses tax deductible? • Resources

Chapter 8—They're only young once!   133

Strengthening family ties • Explaining why you work • Homework for the workaholic • When baby sets your schedule • Surviving the summer while keeping your cool • Keeping in touch while you travel • Running business errands • Easy activities for the little ones • How much TV is too much TV? • When the phone rings • How to be artsy when you're certainly not crafty • Recipes kids can try • "Me work too!" • Finding kids' play things • Resources

Chapter 9—Involving your older children   155

Kids can come in handy! • Finding age-appropriate tasks • Tax advantages • How a good parent can be a great boss • Finding your children's hidden talents • Teaching children about money • Teaching business etiquette • What if my child doesn't want to work for *me*? • Resources

Chapter 10—Redefining yourself   165

"Wait a minute...I work!" • Facing subtle put-downs • So you're expecting? • Finding help while you're away • Moving your business • Why the marital spats? • Money matters • Does divorce affect a home-based business? • 12 tips for nurturing yourself • Exiting one business, entering another • A new look for you • Sanity savers • Good things can happen to you • Resources

Conclusion—Inspiration to get you started   181

Appendix—Resources for work-at-home parents   183

Associations • Newsletters • Software/videos • Web sites

About the author   187

Index   189

The best of both worlds

Growing up in the 70s, I bought into the myth of having it all—a happy marriage, kids, a comfortable home, a rewarding career, and, of course, the healthy paycheck required to support the lifestyle I aspired to. In 1988 when my husband and I welcomed our son Andy into the world, I thought I was well on my way to achieving the dream. I discovered too soon that "having it all" really was more myth than reality.

Like many parents shouldering new responsibilities, I saw first-hand how completely children change one's marital and professional landscape. As much as I wanted to spend more time with the baby and focus on the family, I *wanted* to work, too. I wanted to pursue a career as a writer—work that might make a difference in another person's day.

As the family bill-payer, I felt the weight of our family's financial goals. It wasn't feasible for me to abandon my career. If my husband and I wanted to realize our dream of building a house in the suburbs, my income was necessary. But what was best for me and my husband, our careers, and perhaps our family's finances, wasn't in my son's best interests. I didn't want to bring Andy to day care each morning and see him for only a few hours in the evening. I wanted to be there, to return that first smile and applaud the first step or spoken word.

I struggled with these conflicting priorities and demands. I spent hours each day trying to figure out a way to—if not have it all—have more of a balance.

Finally I came upon a solution: I could work at home! Sure there'd be challenges to launching a home-based career. My income would be uncertain, especially as I built my business. I'd never be away from my work. I'd see paper piles waiting to be tackled, hear the phone ring at private times, and I'd always feel the pressure to accomplish more, make one last call, squeeze in another assignment. Stubborn as ever, equipped with a computer and my can-do attitude, I joined the work-at-home ranks.

I did cut back the income level I'd achieved working full-time. I answered ads, sent out resumes, and shared my goals with anyone who would listen. I admit I felt like I was begging at times. Every day had a certain amount of dread, like a job search, but I discovered another part of me that lay dormant—the part with a love for new, daily discoveries.

Slowly, after once or twice vowing to pursue a career in plumbing, I saw more acceptances than rejections as I submitted my work. The three of us settled into our newly constructed house, and I acclimated to the life of an at-home professional and mom.

Then Alex came along. We'd planned on a second child, but Alex's birth 12 weeks early caught us completely by surprise as he spent two months in the highest level of neonatal intensive care. Thankfully, we all survived the experience, Alex thrived, and my career began to take off. In time, my first book, *Writing for Money,* was published, amid book signings and media attention.

It seemed as if I truly had achieved my girlhood fantasy of "having it all." A few years went by as my husband and I enjoyed a comfortable lifestyle, financial security, and I successfully balanced career and motherhood. Suddenly, my husband announced he was seeking a separation and it appeared our marriage was over.

Talk about a stressful life change! There went the goals and stability that makes working at home easier. Suddenly I felt the full responsibility for taking care of my two boys, the house, the demands of my writing, and now the added toll of the separation. Having it all meant *doing* it all. I was lucky I could keep out from under the snow, much less plan my professional workload.

I thought at first that this juncture might even spell the end of my ability to work from home. At the same time, I could see the staggering effect the marital breakup had on my children, and I knew more than ever that they needed me at home.

The reason I share these fits and starts with you is to convey that I know how hard it is to juggle the *full* responsibility of kids and work. But I've done it, fought some awful fears and distractions, and I've learned a lot of coping strategies. Somehow I hope you'll draw courage from my example and the experiences I share, for if I can do it, so can you. Today, my home-based writing career greets me with new opportunities every morning. I shelve the doubts and realize that working at home and raising a family is what I make of it.

Believe me, I'm not wealthy. I had to cut back my workload to meet the special needs of my children. Even today, as I put the finishing touches on this book you're reading, my youngest woke with an asthma attack. The entire day, including my work schedule, will have to be altered. This often means taking in less work and bringing in less income.

I can let all this overwhelm me, or demonstrate to my two boys that I'm a hard worker as well as a mom doing the best job she can. One of my favorite quotes from my *Think & Grow Rich* calendar reads, "Tell me how you use your spare time and I'll tell you where you'll be in 10 years!"

With this book, I hope to make a difference in your very first—and tenth—year working from home. I'll offer advice, coping mechanisms, and hundreds of tips I've learned about integrating a home-based career with raising an active family.

If you think I have all the answers, I hope you aren't disappointed. There are issues I still struggle with. The only difference is, as a journalist, I have a neurotic need to seek solutions. Like when I had a 30-minute radio interview by phone and my little one was home sick—How does one draw more than a half-hour out of "Barney"? (You'll have to read further for the answer!)

I'll share moments like these and anecdotes that other working moms and dads have offered. I'll respond to common questions and misconceptions with uncommon answers. And I'll provide resources that might help you along your career and parenting paths.

Although I realize that women are more apt to choose a home-based career, plenty of men have chosen to work at home in order to spend more time with their kids. Although I have young children, you may have teens, grown children, or even grandkids that you care for while working. My own experiences may be as a single mother with two young children, but I believe this book will be of great value to any work-at-home caregiver, regardless of gender, age of children, or other circumstances.

Throughout this book I will be respectful of your time. There just isn't enough of it when you're juggling career and children under the same roof. When I started out, work-at-home parents had to read both parenting and business books to get all the guidance they needed. This book is an all-in-one resource.

You *can* work at home when the kids are there, and you don't have to tie up any children in the basement to do so! You might be tempted some days, but I can assure you that string and duct tape aren't necessary to implement this book!

What is necessary is your enthusiasm, along with mine, as we carve out careers that fulfill us, provide for our financial needs, and set creative examples for our children. Grab a cup of coffee (or Kool-Aid), and let's begin!

—Loriann Hoff Oberlin

Chapter 1

Choosing a home-based career

Maybe after reading the introduction to this book, you have a work-at-home idea you're ready to pursue. Maybe you had one before you even bought the book. In either case, congratulations! A good idea ignites the entrepreneurial fire within you. Without such an image, your drive to pursue a home-based career can come to a crashing halt.

A good idea is indeed a crucial first step in launching a successful home-based business. But understand, first, that no matter how outstanding your idea, you must first be sure that working at home is the best choice for you. Think carefully about the pluses and minuses of a home-based career.

On the upside, you'll be your own boss, set your own hours, dress the way you want, commence and complete the day at your choosing. No more battling traffic. No more putting up with people you'd just as soon ignore. No more unproductive meetings or co-workers who won't leave your office.

On the downside, working at home has its challenges—the temptation to slack off and the very real need to discipline yourself every moment of the workday; the casual clothes that might spill over into a casual attitude and approach; the loneliness that comes from working by yourself most of the day, without a soul to complain to or pat you on the back; the insecurity of not knowing where the next client or project will come from.

Before you decide *what* you want to do as a home-based career, you must first be certain that the work-at-home environment is a healthy match for you. Are you self-motivated? Good at setting goals and meeting them? Do you enjoy working independently? These are some of the characteristics that are compatible with working at home. If you have a hard time cracking the whip on yourself, if you struggle to meet deadlines, if you require a lot of direction and motivation from others, then you might want to remain on someone else's payroll, reporting to a boss and meeting prescribed expectations.

Take time to do some self-analysis before you take the plunge. Once you've confirmed that working at home is the solution to your career and family goals, you'll want to explore *what* you'll be doing at home.

Of course there may be no question as to what kind of work you'll do. Perhaps you've been an accountant in the corporate world—the natural transition might be to set up your own accounting practice out of your extra bedroom and launch your business during tax season. Maybe you have been a staff writer for a newspaper or magazine or a copywriter for an advertising agency. Taking your talent home and going freelance might make sense.

But if your work experience is not so easily transferable—or if you just want to do something new—you'll want to explore a variety of options, considering your own special skills and interests as well as business and lifestyle trends. This chapter will offer some ideas, but there's a world of possibilities out there. Keep searching until you discover a satisfying match.

Is telecommuting for you?

Before you put too much emphasis on choosing a new business endeavor, you may want to explore an option that's right. Indeed, changing your status from an office-based staffer to a telecommuter might be the simplest solution.

With the advances of technology, telecommuting has become quite popular as an alternative job arrangement, allowing you to work from home without having to face some of the self-employed fears. With the help of phone lines that tie you to the office via your computer or a fax machine, you can go about your daily work, open and answer electronic mail, and communicate with your colleagues on site. Of course, a major benefit of telecommuting is that you still have the "security" of a steady paycheck and all of the other benefits that go along with having an employer.

Employers have found that telecommuting can increase productivity, especially when workers convert what would have been their commuting time to productive work-related activity. As this concept has caught on, absenteeism has been reduced and so has the cost of recruiting and retraining valuable employees who leave a job in search of more flexible arrangements. It also increases morale and eliminates overhead costs. Essentially, it's easier to buy technology than it is to purchase real estate!

The flipside of this is that telecommuting is still a relatively new concept, often requiring an aggressive posture to sell the idea to an employer. If your employer is hesitant to give the nod, propose a test run, working on a particular project in which your productivity can be measured. (In fact, bosses supervising telecommuters *should* be looking for results rather than worrying about the activity level.)

Employers might also be concerned about your working conditions. The Occupational Safety and Health Administration (OSHA) is in the process of establishing guidelines for telecommuting employees. Rest assured, your employer's obligation to provide a safe workplace does not end at the traditional office. To ease this concern, you might want to work out an agreement establishing safety principles, work hours, and company-owned equipment policies. This can lessen any risk to your employer.

Become computer literate, asking your company's MIS coordinator for help with hardware, operating systems compatibility, transferring files, modems, networking between computers, and any other technological requirements of your job (see Chapter 3). Chances are you will need to become fairly self-sufficient, being connected to the company by computer, since the technological wiz you may have relied upon in the next cubicle will not be as readily available to help you in a crisis.

Even if your work-at home arrangement works successfully and exceeds your expectations, those who've tried it agree that you'll probably need a presence one or two days a week in the company's office. Other ways to strengthen and maintain a telecommuting position?

- Give your boss or supervisor weekly status reports (stress the benefit of *more* communication than may have previously taken place).

- Present a lineup of the upcoming week's activities, including an agenda of things the two of you might need to discuss.

- Pass along pertinent professional articles or timely reading (this shows how you're keeping abreast of the industry).

- Establish hours that you will always be available by phone as this provides consistency (and shows that you may even be more accessible than you were at the on-site office).

- Be upfront about personal days or vacation weeks you'll be taking off so that no one jumps to any conclusions about your absence.

- Always speak in terms such as "I'll be out of my office between 3 and 5 p.m. running business errands." Do not focus on the word "home," but use "office" instead.

Those careers most suited to telecommuting include computer programming and systems analysis, sales, news reporting and writing, public relations work, brokerage, data entry, and translation services. These occupations require less direct contact and bodily presence but rely heavily on independent work involving telephones, fax machines, computers, and other modern communications devices.

What's out there?

The majority of work-at-home opportunities can be broken down into two categories—marketing your services or selling your products. This chapter can't possibly list all the options available to you. For a comprehensive study please refer to the Resources section at the end of the chapter.

There were 30 million work-at-home households in 1996, up from 27.3 million in 1995, according to Raymond L. Boggs, director of the Home Office Research Program at IDC/LINK, a Manhattan-based research firm. Boggs projects that by 2001, that number will be at 44.5 million, reflecting an annual growth rate of 8.5 percent from 1995.

According to Richard Ekstract, of the Home Office Association of America, we're in the midst of an extraordinary workplace transformation. "As we head into the new millennium, the number of home offices will skyrocket," Ekstract says. "The same people who were workaholics and corporate climbers in the 80s now seek personally rewarding and satisfying outlets for their talents. The 'me-first' attitude is being replaced with a more family-oriented mentality."

Trust me, there is a work-at-home career path for you, and one in which you will be able to meet the needs of your children. Whether you are making a product (such as candles, food, artwork, or wooden toys), selling a service (consulting, writing, furniture restoration, hair dressing, or translation), dealing directly with children (with a kids' library, day-care center, or private lessons), or using your car or telephone (conducting surveys, making deliveries, handling special sales), there are hundreds, perhaps thousands of avenues you can explore from your home base.

"Tens of millions of Americans now work in their homes," writes Marshall Loeb in his book *Marshall Loeb's Lifetime Financial Strategies*. "If they make it past the 13th month—the critical test, say home-business consultants—most find rewards in both income and lifestyle. The fastest-growing of these enterprises are computer data and word processing, direct sales for commissions, and general business services, including accounting, bookkeeping, and typing."

Whichever opportunity you choose, realize the benefits as well as the drawbacks. The clear picture depends upon an honest assessment and how you look at any given idea. What's right for one home worker might not be appropriate for you, and what seems totally impossible with toddlers at home might be viable as your children get older.

Become a trend spotter

As you explore what sort of business to offer from home, it's important to have your finger on the pulse of the public. Where does the world seem to be heading? Look at the trends that are hot now and promise to burn even brighter. Look at what businesses are booming.

In order to become a trend spotter, read books, peruse the daily paper, and pull out magazine articles to save. Some publications I've found particularly helpful in spotting trends include *People* magazine and *USA Today,* with its "USA Snapshots" column, a daily dose of new and trendy information. See if your newsstand or library carries *Futurist* or *American Demographics,* which keep tabs on consumer trends. Authors such as John Naisbitt, Faith Popcorn, and Alvin Toffler also offer valuable insights in their books.

Listen to talk radio, televised interviews, and newscasts. Tune in to the comedy channel and listen to comedic monologues. While you may argue the newsworthiness of these, you'll certainly learn what's getting people to laugh and react. As you're out shopping, browse the racks of greeting cards. Writers of these funny sentiments survive by spotting popular trends and buzzwords. In a sense, they've done a lot of research for you.

To know what's hot, pay attention—observe. That is how most people find their business niche and decide how they'll fill it.

Finally, look to your own situation—your needs and lifestyle demands—for ideas and inspiration. Another mom I know began publishing a newsletter—*NICU News*—for parents with children in the neonatal unit. She saw a lack of information when her son was born, and she decided to fill the void for others.

The bottom line

Before you decide upon your business or career path, determine how much you'll have to invest in start-up costs. A greeting-card writer can set herself up with a stack of index cards, some envelopes, stamps, a notebook, and a typewriter. Someone who sells Discovery Toys or another demonstration-oriented product might need to invest several hundred dollars in a kit. A dentist or physician who converts a portion of his or her home to use as a worksite will incur thousands of dollars worth of expenses for equipment, licenses, remodeling, and more.

How to assess your skills

Career counseling is a very valuable service, available through a variety of sources. One choice is to return to your high school guidance counselor or career planning director of your college or university. Some pastoral counseling centers around the country also offer this assessment.

If you face downsizing or dismissal from your current position, request outplacement services. Most outplacement firms use a series of psychological and standardized measures to assess your needs, skills, and talents. "The key variables you want to look at are aptitudes (i.e., your transferable skills), your interests, and your personality and motivational factors," says Murray D. Thompson, Ph.D., of the outplacement firm Collins Thompson Consulting Group in Monroeville, Pa. According to Thompson, the typical entrepreneur fits this psychological profile with:

- Strong dominance needs, meaning a preference to control the variables that affect him or her.

- Moderately high achievement needs.

- Relatively high needs for organizational autonomy, that is, the ability to function independent of structure.

- Strong affiliation needs that surface in socially bold people who need interaction with others.

- A sense of self-sufficiency, resourcefulness, and self-discipline.

Thompson presents the results from the assessments to his clients individually, explaining each finding. Testing is especially helpful when it's completed with the aid of a psychologist who can offer feedback. One popular test is the Myers-Briggs Type Indicator® (MBTI) which is based upon the work of noted behaviorist C.G. Jung. The test indicates whether you are more extroverted or introverted, sensing or intuitive, thinking or feeling, and judging or perceiving. The MBTI reveals your preferences, not necessarily your skills.

As with any service you seek, choose a career counselor carefully. Richard Nelson Bolles, in his book *What Color Is Your Parachute?*, lists some career counselors around the country and warns what you should watch out for. Beware of counselors who insist upon payment up front. You shouldn't have to sign a contract or pay advanced fees. You should be able to pay as you go, at the end of each counseling session, and be able to terminate sessions at any time. In fact, you might want to peruse Bolles' book, listed with some other excellent resources at the end of this chapter. It's a valuable guide with chapters and exercises on skill assessment.

What to do when you're downsized

Global competition, business deregulation, corporate mergers, and acquisitions have affected thousands of employees, many of whom no longer believe in the idea of job security. And the trend doesn't seem to be abating. Whether you've been let go in a downsizing posture, or terminated for some other reason, let it propel you into successful self-employment.

Some companies will offer you outplacement counseling, and even if you're pretty set on establishing your own company, my suggestion would be to go through the outplacement process. You have nothing to lose and everything to gain. Psychologically it might help identify any anger, fear and self-doubt about your job loss, and it will empower you to take charge of your future. Such counseling usually includes an assessment of your interests, values, and personality characteristics. This will tell you if you're correctly suited to self-employment, whether you should seriously reconsider, or choose another option.

If you're offered a severance package, this is an added bonus, and a sum of money you can invest in your new venture. If you are an information professional or consultant, however, you won't have the high start-up costs that a product-oriented business might. For instance, someone setting up their own mechanic shop would require more of a capital investment for equipment, materials, and supplies.

Beside counseling and finances, the next crucial step is finding clients and building your professional network. If you've thought ahead, and managed your career well thus far, chances are good you already have name recognition in your field and a healthy Rolodex to show it. Cultivate these resources. Often your own employer or clients will retain your services as you make the transition from an employee on payroll to the ranks of the self-employed.

If you're fortunate enough to see the change in your career approaching, there are definite steps you can take to get your new business off to a successful start. Apply for financing before you are terminated. Write a solid business plan. Get yourself known through giving speeches, writing articles, talking to associates, and always reaching out to help others.

In addition, conserve cash. This isn't the time to splurge on nonessentials. In fact, you should stash away six to 12 months of living expenses until you can produce a steady cash flow.

Look at how much income you'll need to generate. If your home-based career is in addition to another job or to the income a working spouse earns, you might be able to get by with less, at least in the beginning. But if your career is the sole support of yourself and your family, your numbers need to be high. Select a career that affords that potential. And don't be surprised if what you actually earn is less than your original estimate. This is very typical of start-up operations.

What business should I pursue? A dozen determining factors

To discover what you're good at and which career paths you'll be most satisfied with, consider carefully this list of questions:

What do I like to work with—people, products and things, or information and analysis?

What do I know about? What am I an expert in?

What do I feel totally inept at? Will this be a part of my career?

How much time is required? How much time do I have to spare?

Can I work while I'm with my children? Or will my work require separating from them for a few hours, an entire day, or longer?

Will my local zoning regulations allow me to work from home?

How long will it take me to start running with this? How much preparation and down time can I afford?

Who else is providing a similar product or service near me?

What makes bringing business to me attractive to clients or customers? If I were in their shoes, would I walk away?

Who do I know who can help me along the way? Do I have any favors to call in? What other resources will I need?

Will I need to hire employees or outside contractors?

Am I in this for the immediate future or the long haul?

Fostering family support

Many entrepreneurs start out with high expectations and solid backing from family and friends. New business starts are generally a source of pride, even the topic of cocktail conversations. But the novelty almost always wears off when your family becomes plagued by late hours and missed meals. Your kids may become disgruntled, your spouse resentful. Of course, you insist, they'll have to be understanding that launching a new business requires sacrifices by all. But be sure of this: Without the steadfast support of a spouse, children, and others close to you, failure becomes a very real factor.

Sit down with your whole family. Share your dreams. Then ask what their concerns might be. You may be surprised to find how easily misconceptions go away with a little communication. Promise your family that you'll step back occasionally and analyze how things are working for all parties involved—and follow through. Encourage them to talk and point out red flags that escape you—like missed traditions, nights out together, relationships, or health issues. If you all agree to air these concerns before communication breaks down and resentment sets in, everyone will go into the arrangement with pride.

Seek involvement as well as support. Ask for input and ideas, calling upon talents you can tap. Your children would probably be delighted to suggest names for your business, select a design or color for your business cards, or search the Web or computer clip art files for appropriate graphics. If family members feel they're contributing to your success and to the family's future, they'll buy into the work-at-home lifestyle. (See Chapter 9.)

Let your family know how much this arrangement means to you, in terms of finances, flexibility, and self-esteem. Tell them you'll never forsake your role as parent or partner. Your job will be there in the morning, but tonight's dinner party or school concert will pass by only once. Promise that you'll relax, take the time to clear your head, and close the door leading to your desk.

Fostering family support calls upon your mastery of gentle persuasion. It's a skill you'll use many times in the days ahead. As my friend Pam Price told me, "I couldn't handle this business without my family sometimes." Pam used to work as a full-time interior designer before beginning her businesses, Celebrations By Design and Basket Styles.

In fact, Pam credits family with the inspiration and ongoing involvement in her businesses. "My sister was the real impetus in my starting up," she admits. "After I'd given a graduation party for my son, she pulled me aside and said, 'People don't normally give parties like this. Why don't you do this for a living?'" Now, years later, Pam's husband, Bob, handles accounting and computer operations. Her father comes in to help with paperwork and billing, and her mother continually passes along tips and useful information. Pam's two children (sometimes their friends as well) have pitched in also.

Avoiding work-at-home scams

Those who find it hard to hold down even a part-time job are often lured by advertisements that promise *huge* profits for a work-at-home project for which there is *great demand. Little or no experience* is necessary. Please *rush* your inquiry so you can cash in.

I've italicized certain words here for a reason. If you're holding an ad that contains similar mentions, you might want to crumble it in your fist. Most work-at-home schemes have two common denominators: They sound too good to be true, and they require you to buy something in advance.

Therein lies the catch. "There's usually just a telephone number to call," warns Jennifer Boerio, vice president of communications for the Better Business Bureau of Western Pennsylvania. "Then, literature comes with the need for you to buy a kit." Boerio tells of one woman who, after sending away for a jewelry kit, assembled beads with the promise that the company would buy her hand-crafted items. When she tried to follow through on that promise, she found that her work suddenly didn't meet quality control standards. This woman was out her money and time, and she had many pairs of earrings to unload.

Watch, also, for schemes that require you to recruit others for the same business plan they are pitching to you. Illegal pyramid-scheme operators take on cheap product lines with no established value. They make no real effort to sell the product but make money recruiting more distributors instead.

Don't be confused by smooth-talking organizers who build your excitement in a plan, then ask you to invest large fees. Check with others who have experience with the company or products. Ask if the company buys back unsold inventory. Other signs of potential trouble: The company is out of town and uses an unlisted telephone number. Legitimate companies do not hide themselves. In fact, you can usually find local companies who are looking to back up their support services (stuffing envelopes and such). Contact your local BBB or state attorney general's office if in doubt.

Providing in-home childcare

Watching other people's kids while you watch yours might be a great way to combine your work and family goals. There are a lot of advantages. Patricia C. Gallagher walked away from her position as an account executive with AT&T in order to spend more time with her own children. But realizing the need for additional income, she put her bachelor's degree in education to good use, launching an at-home childcare business in her home. The decision eliminated gas, lunch, wardrobe, and her own childcare expenses. It also required little cash outlay.

"The childcare business gives you almost immediate profit because you are paid on a regular basis," writes Gallagher in *Start Your Own At-Home Child Care Business.* "Although you may need baby equipment, toys, and some other supplies, you will be pleasantly surprised to find that your friends and relatives have lots of used items that they would be glad to pass on to help get you started in your new venture." Gallagher's other thoughts for would-be childcare providers:

- Seek training, especially CPR, rescue breathing, and first aid classes.
- Childproof your home, removing fragile, dangerous, and small items that could be swallowed. Crawl around on the floor to find hazards.
- Contact state licensing boards and conform to any local requirements.
- Hire help for busy times, especially nap time and mealtime.
- Invest in the equipment and supplies you need. Get a cordless telephone so you can constantly keep an eye on the children.
- Don't take on more children than you can handle. Set age requirements if you must.
- Provide a daily routine that's warm and creative. Check out libraries, playgrounds, or other field trip sights in advance (noting rest rooms, parking, etc.). Encourage a child's curiosity with arts and crafts, story-telling, lessons, and more.
- Network with other at-home caregivers. Seek additional training and subscribe to pertinent publications. (See Resources in this chapter).

Money-making ideas

Still stuck on finding a home-based career? One thing is for sure: Choose a job or task people hate to do for themselves, and you will have customers! Find out what troubles most people, and how you might be able to alleviate some of their fears and frustrations. Where there is pain, there is gain—for you! Peruse the following list of opportunities for one that's right for you:

- Administrative assistance: Support services are in great demand. If you can develop and maintain databases, assist with mailings, or provide last-minute secretarial help, you could have a very busy business.

- Arts & crafts: Turn a hobby into a business, making and selling artwork, baskets, crafts, pottery, and more.

- Completing tax returns: This field keeps you busy nonstop from January through April 15, but winds down for the rest of the year.

- Makeovers: Offer to do makeovers for bridal parties, television studios, photographers, or others who need your expertise. Advertise using before and after photographs, displayed in bridal shops and studios.

- Home inspections: Inspect hazards and install safeguards for new parents who need a childproofed home. Inspect homes for real estate companies and banks before sales can go through. If your background is in police work or security, sell your services to homeowners concerned about their house's vulnerability to burglars.

- Home repair: Today's busy homeowner doesn't have the time to tackle routine repair jobs, and he or she hesitates to spend bundles on the job, going to the top professionals. So if you have a flair for repair, this could lead to reasonable income.

- Growing herbs and produce: Love to garden? Grow these in your backyard, selling them at farmer's or flea markets.

- Typing resumes and papers: Especially if you have desktop publishing equipment, typing resumes, cover letters, term papers, and theses for job seekers and students can result in extra money. Advertise in student newspapers or sell your credentials to established printers or resume writing services.

- Tutoring: Dust off that undergraduate degree and put it to good use sharing what you know about a particular subject, musical instrument, or sport. Advertise in local newspapers or bargain guides. Post flyers at libraries. Let teachers and principals know what you offer.

- Home computer consulting: What about all those people who purchase or receive new computers for Christmas? Without the help of someone who can hook up the system, get it running, and give a little instruction, that hefty purchase may simply sit in the box.

- Web site development: Sure, major corporations can afford top design professionals, but small businesses and entrepreneurs scramble to find assistance at the right price. If you can prepare text, integrate graphics, and maintain the sites, this could be a thriving business for you.

- Pleasing parents: If you like the thought of helping other families while spending more time with your own, you could begin a personalized book service, provide photography for special occasions, a diaper delivery service, or individual swimming lessons (if you have a pool). Out-of-the-home opportunities exist if you could chaperone children at bus stops, become a *doula,* providing postpartum care for moms and new babies, or even cook and deliver meals for new moms or families that don't have much time for meal preparation.

- Selling home-demonstration products: If you only have evenings available, demonstrate and sell educational toys, cleaning products, home accessories, encyclopedias, and more.

- Party planning: We all love going to parties, but like speaking in public, planning them is a task that frightens many of us. If you love coordinating color schemes, deciding upon menus, making favors, and working to create just the right atmosphere, you can help individuals or businesses celebrate special events.

- Providing entertainment: If you love to elicit a laugh, clown around for cash, sing, dance, do magic tricks, or paint kid's faces. With a little creativity, you can perform for children's parties, and community and school groups.

- Being a paralegal: In today's litigious society, the paralegal business is booming. Set yourself up with Lexis, the legal online service, and you can attract business from time-pressed attorneys or small businesses who want to keep their legal fees to a minimum.

- Creating a coffee cart: Serve beverages, bagels, and donuts to office workers mid-morning. Then you're done for the day.

- Putting your car or van to work: Shuttle children to ballgames and band practice, elderly adults to shopping malls and doctor's appointments, or business travelers and vacationers to the airport. Put your lawnmower and gardening tools in the trunk and begin a landscaping business.

Resources

Writing for Money by Loriann Hoff Oberlin (Writer's Digest Books).

101 Best Weekend Businesses by Dan Ramsey (Career Press).

101 Best Home Businesses by Dan Ramsey (Career Press).

The Best Home Businesses for The 90s by Paul and Sarah Edwards (Tarcher/Putnam).

Making Money with Your Computer At Home by Paul and Sarah Edwards (Tarcher/Putnam).

Make Money with Your Computer by Lynn Walford (Ten Speed Press).

Money In Your Mailbox: How to Start and Operate a Successful Mail-Order Business by L. Perry Wilbur (Wiley).

How to Develop & Promote Successful Seminars & Workshops by Howard L. Shenson (Wiley).

Kiplinger's Working for Yourself by Joseph Anthony (Kiplinger Books).

Out of Work? Get Into Business! by Don Doman (Self-Counsel Press).

Fired Up: From Corporate Kiss-Off to Entrepreneurial Kick-Off by Michael Gill and Sheila Paterson (Viking).

The Virtual Office Survival Handbook by Alice Bredin (Wiley).

1101 Businesses You Can Start from Home by Daryl Allen Hall (Wiley).

What Color Is Your Parachute? by Richard Nelson Bolles (Ten Speed Press).

The Smart Woman's Guide to Networking by Betsy Sheldon and Joyce Hadley (Career Press).

How to Start a Home-Based Craft Business by Kenn Oberrecht (Globe Pequot).

Crafting for Dollars by Sylvia Landman (Prima).

How to Open and Operate a Home-Based Day-Care Business by Shari Steelsmith (Globe Pequot).

Pay Dirt: How to Raise and Sell Herbs and Produce for Serious Cash by Mimi Luebbermann (Prima).

Start Your Own At-Home Child Care Business by Patricia C. Gallagher (Young Sparrow Press).

The Smart Woman's Guide to Starting a Business by Vickie Montgomery (Career Press).

Self-Counsel Press "Start & Run Series" of books with step-by-step business plans.

Chapter 2

Launching your business

Somewhere during your first day at work, the reality will suddenly hit. Not only are you minding the phones, the files, and the accounting ledgers, but you're even taking out the trash!

Unlike in a traditional workplace, where you're focused on *your* job only, you'll discover as an at-home businessperson that you're responsible for it all. That may include seeking financing, keeping the books, answering the phones, creating a marketing plan, writing and designing advertisements and direct mail pieces, purchasing and maintaining office equipment, handling correspondence, answering the door for the delivery service, faxing, copying, and, of course, making the coffee.

On top of all this, you have the added challenge of raising a family under the same roof. The kids will only yell louder to get your attention! Rest assured, the telephone will ring with that all important call-back as soon as baby is strapped in the high-chair.

So without the support and structure that corporate professionals have, you'll need to manage all aspects of successfully launching your new business. That's what this chapter is about. Attitude is everything. You *can* successfully get your business off the ground and manage your business responsibilities while you juggle the family agenda. Sure you'll have days when you'll be tempted to chuck the work-at-home concept for corporate America, but when that moment occurs, switch on the news—the traffic snarls and downsizing headlines will probably temper your mood.

There's no way I can tell you everything you need to know in order to launch your business. There are books and college courses on the topic. Read as much as you can about business startups (there are some great books in the resource section of this chapter to get you started), especially on the topics of writing a business plan, seeking financing, and developing your sales and marketing efforts.

To round out your knowledge, I've gathered advice and tips on a variety of key issues that may be important to you as a work-at-home parent starting up a new enterprise. These include everything from nuts-and-bolts issues, such as getting your office in order to emotional concerns, such as the fear of failure.

Business plans that win you the work

Imagine a construction crew attempting to erect a house without the benefit of a blueprint. Where will they put the boards? Do they build straight up or dig a wider foundation? Before the cement truck pours concrete and the first board is ever nailed, it helps to have a plan. So it is with your business venture.

Your bankers or investors will require a business plan before they consider financing your venture. You may not know exactly where you'll end up in five, 10, or 20 years, but you should at least have some ideas. You can use these ideas to measure your success along the way.

Begin your business plan with a *one- to three-page summary*. Don't write a bland, passive account, but remember to use the active voice, and use carefully chosen verbs that deliver impact. Your summary should detail:

- What your business venture, product or service will do for others.
- How it will be financed.
- How it will be organized.
- Who will be its customers.
- Who will be its suppliers.
- How you will promote your venture (see Chapter 5).

Following your summary, prepare three more-detailed sections:

1. **A market overview** that details who will buy your product or service, at what price, and why.
2. **A financial discussion** that explains exactly how money will be raised and spent, as well as an estimate of how long it will take your venture to turn a profit.
3. **Biographies** of yourself and other owners or managers, that answer investors' questions including, "Why should I lend this person money for this venture?" Focus on experience and expertise—in other words, what you bring to the table, not what you'll take away from it.

Create a *projected income statement* showing all anticipated sources of revenue and expenses, and a *balance sheet* that lists projected assets and liabilities. Include a *five-year forecast of cash flow* to show whether you can continue to meet the operating expenses you'll face. Don't underestimate, especially in areas of marketing, legal, and accounting services, for which you'll need cash outlays.

When you have what you feel is an acceptable plan, treat it as a rough draft. Revise it. Tighten the wording. Make each sentence and each word work, and move your plan forward in the reader's mind. Don't hesitate to create customized versions of the same business plan. These individualized plans follow the same framework, but more directly answer the concerns of various readers—bankers, other investors, managers, employees, yourself.

Your plan should be neatly typed with plenty of white space to make it more readable. Place the numbered pages into a presentation folder of your choice, preferably one that holds a business card.

Refer to the Resources section of this chapter to discover more detailed information on preparing a business plan.

Naming your business

The name under which you choose to operate your business is your first signal to the world that you're ready to work. Although many at-home workers don't create a name for their business, promoting themselves under their name (Loriann Hoff Oberlin, writer), a business name is an advantage for most businesses—if only to create a compelling listing in the yellow pages. Consider these factors:

- What are the benefits of your product or service? Does your personal shopping service *free up valuable time* for your clients? Does your resume writing service put your customer *in line for a better job*? Does your tax-preparation service increase the possibility of a *bigger tax return* to your market? Identifying the *benefits,* not just the features, of your business might bring to light a powerful phrase or word that will convey value to prospects when they read your name.

- Create a name that is descriptive yet flexible enough for future growth. When I first began writing for *Elegant Bride* magazine, the publication was titled *Southern Bride.* But that name limited its scope. It didn't take the publisher long to enhance the magazine's image with a better name.

- Think subconsciously. If your last name is Wilton, you would not want to name your floral shop "Wilton's Flowers."

- Think internationally. There have been some marketing horror stories about American products, which, when translated into foreign languages, produced embarrassing phrases. When Chevrolet introduced its Nova in Mexico, consumers were understandably reluctant to buy a brand that, when translated into Spanish, was called, "It doesn't go."

- Eliminate "the" or "a" from the name, if you can—"House of Dolls" instead of "The House of Dolls." The definite article adds nothing but additional letters that take up space on your business card, stationery, and promotional pieces.

- Although a clever business name will certainly attract more attention and earn you points for being witty, never sacrifice meaning. A straightforward name will always serve you better than something that doesn't clearly identify what service or product you offer. For example, although "Resume Service" doesn't have much pizzazz, it's much clearer to the customer what you're offering than "Do the Write Thing."

- As for using your surname, the shorter your last name, the better. Think twice before using hyphenated or lengthy names as well as those that are difficult to spell or pronounce.

Once you've settled on a name you're happy with, call the office of the secretary of state in your state capitol. Ask for a quick computer search of all incorporated businesses to see if anyone already operates under that name. Actually, it's wise to check all states just in case you expand your horizons. Register your name with your city or county clerk to protect against others using it. You'll also need to publish notice of it in general-circulation newspapers.

Because each of these subjects could be the focus of books themselves, and because laws vary from state to state, I'd suggest doing some reading and research on your own first. Start by obtaining the complete catalog of self-help legal books published by Nolo Press. It's full of resources on patents, copyrights, trademarks, and more. Call 800-992-6656.

Business cards and stationery

After you've established your business name, hire a freelance graphic designer (or do it yourself if you have the talent and inclination) to make your name work visually. You'll want to use both the name and logo on business cards, stationery, envelopes, invoices, and advertising to reinforce your image. This is the most effective form of advertising.

Any print shop or printing department at an office supply center can advise you when it comes to ordering these items, but as you launch your business, you will most certainly need a supply of basic stationery. Your best bet is to shop around for quality of work and a good price. Ask other small business owners for their recommendations. Or browse through sample books that most printers display with work they've produced.

If you can provide camera-ready artwork to your printer, it will save you money. With so many of us having a desktop publishing program or other software to use, creating artwork can be a fun part of the start-up process. If family members can help, even more people are happy. Just be certain things appear the way you want them.

Each time you ask the printer to move a line or change a letter, you're adding to your bill. Analyze what you really want in your promotional printing, and play with the options at home, on the screen, before involving a printer.

Many printers extend discounts if you use standard colors and are not in a hurry to complete your job. You might just save yourself set-up costs if you go with a standard ink that's on press each week. The more custom colors you add, the more you should expect to pay.

For additional tips on creating business cards and letterhead, read Chapter 5 on promotion.

Setting your hours

I often tell beginning freelance writers to choose whatever time they are freshest to devote to the business of writing. That same advice may work for you—or it may not. When you have children, you frequently cannot pick your ideal work time. You're at the mercy of your children's schedules, be it nap time, nursery school, the schedule of the school bus, or soccer practice.

I can't tell you when to work. That has to be your decision, based upon your work and your family demands. However, I can give you some ideas that will allow you to squeeze in chunks of work here and there.

Many home-based entrepreneurs enjoy the solitude of early morning hours when the house is quiet. Showered and dressed, or merely in slippers and robe, they go to their desks with a cup of coffee to read over the paper in peace, have the computer to themselves, or undertake some other essential business activity.

Others prefer to get the kids on the school bus before they tackle any serious work at hand. The beauty of working at home means that you can use those valuable hours your corporate counterparts are commuting to your best advantage. Lunch hour is treated the same way. Although it's beneficial to get out of your office for the occasional business lunch, it can be equally useful to catch a bite at your desk while you make use of the time.

The advantage, of course, to a home-based business, is that you have the flexibility to set your hours at your convenience. This means you can take care of personal responsibilities, such as grocery shopping, banking, or getting a haircut, when the crowds are fewer.

However, because you want to be convenient to your clients, it is wise to establish some sort of window of availability in which they know they can reach you. Sure you can work on your client's corporate brochure at 6 a.m. when you're freshest, but if you're always out to the store or taking the kids to the pool when they try to call you during the day, your clients will soon become frustrated and look elsewhere for help.

If you provide a service to the business community, it will make sense to set your business hours during the traditional workday. You might establish, for example, that you will typically be available for meetings or phone calls Monday through Friday between 9 a.m. and 2 p.m. Or if your afternoons are more predictable, noon to 5 p.m. Of course, you'll be working more hours than established, but your clients will always know that they can reach you during these set times. If you do have to be away during these times on occasion, you'll want to be sure to check messages frequently and return calls promptly.

Smart financial strategies

1. Start out with an emergency fund

The astute business owner keeps a cash reserve on hand that equals three to six months of operating expenses, or more, to survive the inevitable down spells. In my own field of freelance writing, editors move to other publications, mergers swallow up some publishers, and some magazines decide to go quarterly rather than publish six issues a year. No matter the industry, circumstances change and there are stagnant periods in which your work—and income—will slow. So prepare for these by having cash on hand, safely tucked away in a money market or savings account.

Learn to operate your business on a budget, and do not deviate from it. Throughout this book you will learn ways to conserve cash, stash savings, and succeed at both money and time management over the long haul. (See Chapter 6 for more details.)

2. Price your products or services carefully

Your research should have indicated what competitors charge. If there are no others near you, try this formula: Estimate how much you would like or need to earn per week. Divide that number by half the number of hours you can realistically put in, and that will put a rate on your time. Why use only half the number of hours in the rate on your time. Why use only half the number of hours in the equation? Because some of your time will be eaten up with administrative, marketing, even clerical tasks.

If this doesn't seem right to you, you might develop pricing that's more expensive for some services, less for others. Or you might come up with a for-profit rate and a not-for-profit rate. Product-based entrepreneurs can base the price of their services on the cost of their materials, plus a mark-up for profit. And still others can price according to what the market will bear. If you offer something truly unique, and there is unlimited demand for it, you can essentially name your price. Or you could set your rates according to perceived-value pricing, a more progressive method.

Sadly, most small business owners do not ask the price they truly deserve. While you may think quoting a lower price helps you bring in business, you may regret that decision over the long haul, wishing you would have charged more.

Any way you figure it, pricing is critical to your long-range success. If you're giving your time (product) away too cheaply, or likewise, if you price yourself out of any sales, you won't stay in business very long.

Tax implications of home businesses

You have latitude when it comes to writing off certain expenses, but you will have to carefully track expenses and records, pay your share (and the employer's share) of Social Security taxes, and file estimated taxes along the way. You'll also have to shop for healthcare coverage and wear many other hats, including the one of chief financial officer. Many entrepreneurs feel the benefits of self-employment outweigh the added tasks of record-keeping and paperwork.

Indeed, some of the tax ramifications of running a home business can be beneficial. After all, you're paying to heat, cool, and insure your home anyway. If you can deduct some of these costs—along with a percentage of your mortgage payment and other utilities—you're better off financially. Then there's that equipment you had to purchase to get up and running. By depreciating these items over a span of years, you can deduct these costs as well.

Zoning, permits, and other important considerations

Most home-based workers should be aware of local zoning laws. You may discover that your community prohibits you from running a business from your home. "Who will know?" you may argue. "It's not like I'm planning to put a neon sign in my front yard." But do you plan to have a volume of clients driving in and out of your driveway? Will delivery trucks be dropping off large shipments in your garage or delivering and picking up packages several times a day? These signs communicate to your neighbors as loudly and clearly as any neon sign that your home is open for business. And this could spell trouble for you if someone were to report it.

It's unfortunate that most of these ordinances were written years ago, and are severely outdated for today's business and economic environment. But with the heightened media attention given to telecommuting, entrepreneurship, and home-based businesses, many communities are updating their laws.

Obtain a copy of the zoning regulations (available at your city hall or library), find out the zone you're in, and read the pertaining passages. Also check any restrictive covenants that apply to your housing plan or apartment building. If you find you are not in compliance with current code, but aren't creating any problems for your neighbors (increased traffic, appointments, and deliveries), you can either work quietly and hope no one notices, or you can apply for a variance or special exemption. To do this, your neighbors will be informed and there will be a public hearing where you can state your views. Worst-case scenario, you'll be found in violation and asked to cease activity. Within the United States, there are generally no financial penalties when this happens. Of course, with the trend toward working from home, you might want to organize others to effect change in the laws.

Inquire about local business registration to see if you need any special permits or licenses. Your city or county clerk or local council has this information. If your business is food-related, you'll be subject to health department guidelines and restrictions. Some states have occupational licenses for certain careers such as accountants, photographers, cosmetologists, and repairers.

Investigate patents, copyrights, and trademarks. Books have been written on these subjects, and an attorney can walk you through the particulars.

If you operate as a sole proprietor, you may never need a lawyer to help organize your business. But if you establish a partnership or corporation, legal assistance is a given. Since every policy is different, consult your insurance carrier regarding business equipment and supplies, and liability coverage. Sometimes just adding a personal umbrella policy decreases personal risk.

Working at Home While the Kids Are There, Too

Remember those expenses you used to incur just to enjoy your favorite hobby, like maybe, books and magazines for the writer, or gardening tools and mulch to tend your herb garden? Turn that hobby into a home business, and those expenses quickly become useful in lowering your tax liability.

According to the IRS, your hobby is looked upon as a business if you have set yourself up to make a profit; maintained careful records; devoted a substantial amount of time to the activity; withdrawn from another professional capacity to take on this particular activity; and earned a profit for three out of five years. Otherwise your operation will be deemed as a hobby, and your expenses will not work to your advantage.

Home office scrutiny

It's true that home businesses and the home office deduction, in particular, raise red flags for a possible audit. However, only a small percentage of tax returns are ever analyzed. My cousin who is a CPA tells me he usually recommends taking the deduction (providing you meet the criteria).

To deduct a portion of your home, you must use that space regularly and exclusively for business activity. This exclusive-use provision means no daybeds, kitchen tables, or other equipment used for activities outside your business. It needs to be a dedicated space that is separate from the rest of your home. This means it must have a door that separates, or at the very least, a partition that sets it off from other areas.

Measure the square footage of your total living space, then measure the square footage of your office. Divide the square footage of your office by the total square footage of your home. If you use tax preparation software or have a CPA do your tax return, this is an easy calculation. Then you'll know that 5 or 10 or whatever percentage of your space is deductible for home-office expenses. If you legitimately qualify for the deduction, you're entitled to it. If you keep adequate records, and you document your home office with photographs, logs, or floor plans depicting the space, you can back up your claim in the event of an audit.

Finding tax advice

Like any professional you hire around your home, personal referrals are about the best route to pursue when searching for advice. If you don't know other home workers who could recommend a tax adviser, check with professionals in peer or networking groups, or simply call your bank or attorney for suggestions. If you are new to an area, call or write your state's society of CPAs, and they should be able to provide a list of certified public accountants near you.

Don't settle on the first adviser to express interest in the job. Do a little homework. First find out if he or she is familiar with your type of business. If you need to educate him or her at the get-go, this rather negates the convenience of seeking professional counsel. Second, there needs to be a personal connection. As in all endeavors, you hit it off with some people and don't with others. Make sure that your tax advisor understands your business goals. If you go to an initial meeting, and the potential advisor immediately imparts suggestions, without listening to your mission and needs, I'd question the viability of this relationship.

Select an accountant who understands you, listens to you, and is up-front about her practices or fees. You can learn from this trusted advisor's experience such things as how to handle company cars, home-office deductions, travel and other expenses, taking a personal salary, and managing the financial aspects of your home business.

The more you can do on your own to keep the costs of professional services to a bare minimum—in this case, keeping careful records and doing simple bookkeeping yourself—the better off you'll be. Use your tax advisor to counsel you on improving your business and personal financial picture, not for clerical or bookkeeping tasks.

What's hot, what's not?

If you've always relied upon others to maintain the books, tax records, and receipts, you may question just what you need to save, and what's worthy of the circular file. When in doubt, *don't* throw it out. Better to hang on to twice the receipts you'll need, pitching them at tax time, than wish you'd have been more organized.

Any receipt that reflects a cost of doing business is worthy of your attention. The easiest way to gauge what is necessary is to look at the expenses traditionally allowed by the Internal Revenue Service. Grab hold of IRS Schedule C (Profit & Loss). Of course, most businesses have their own unique expenses. Such items as memberships, postage or other categories peculiar to your field are worth adding at the end.

Some home workers will have a high enough volume to organize their receipts, and determine their profit or loss on a monthly basis. As a freelance writer, I've found it convenient to categorize expenses quarterly, setting aside time every three months to total the costs of my writing business. Quarterly analysis also makes sense if you must pay estimated taxes to the IRS, state and local municipality, and most self-employed people will have to do this. If you haven't yet, write or call these revenue collections offices and ask for the appropriate paperwork. They'll place you on the mailing list, and you'll receive the forms and envelopes to submit each subsequent year.

In addition to receipts, calendars and log books are equally useful. Not only will your calendar tell you what went on any given day, but it might support your equipment usage, mileage records and telephone bill. The more corroborating evidence you have, the better off you'll be if you should lose information or be audited by the IRS.

Getting organized

On a scale of one to 10, rating the need for organization and neatness, I'd rank myself around nine. But the first lesson I learned about managing a career one minute and tending to the family the next is to become a little like Gumby—bend and stretch.

Getting organized, though, as you launch your new business is crucial not only to your day-to-day efficiency but your long-term success as well. Sure, you can have your day, even week, month, or year planned out to the hour—and you can count on something happening to bring your smoothly running operation to a screeching halt. Your child wakes up with red spots all over his face. The kids' carpool cancels. A last-minute school project requires a special trip to the library. But by having that organizational structure in place, you'll fall back into efficient operation once the immediate crisis is over.

Setting your hours, establishing your goals, and organizing your files are all components of an organizational structure that will keep you on track, despite those numerous interruptions, surprises, and family disasters that you can count on. Here are just a few tips to get you going:

Set long-term and short-term goals

Most businesses (and perhaps you've worked for some) establish one-year goals, five-year goals, and even 10-year goals. But in order to achieve these long-range marks, they know the importance of setting smaller, short-term goals, breaking up the journey into shorter trips that get them closer, mile by mile, to their ultimate destination.

You can do the same. If, for example, your goal is to be on retainer with five large corporate clients within three years, your interim goals might be to identify 20 corporations you want to make initial contact with within the next six months. Or to be working regularly with two corporate clients within the year. Or to get three referrals each from your current clients.

If you set goals periodically, this process is less burdensome. If you're like me, you think of major goals annually, but later adapt your plans on a quarterly, or even a monthly basis. Either way, you find yourself working toward something—each day—instead of not working at all.

Get your files in order

Keeping proper records can be easily forgotten when the harried business owner juggles work and family responsibilities. Organization never seems a priority, what with a deadline looming, clients to call back, and dinner to make. But you must maintain some system, even a primitive one, where your business data is filed away and you know how to retrieve it. You can always go back and weed out unnecessary paperwork or delete outdated computer files.

Because so many professionals use computers today, I believe a balance of electronic files and hard copy is necessary. One backs the other up. On those occasions you can't find the printout, it's reassuring to know you can probably locate the material you need on a floppy disk.

Avoid computer crisis and information loss

Get into the habit of backing up your projects after each work session. It only takes a minute to insert a floppy disk and protect your work. To further minimize the risk of losing important files and data, I always recommend making periodic system backups of your computer hard drive. As boring as it may seem to keep inserting and labeling disks for two hours straight, it's worth it if you must replace the information. In the interest of time, take advantage of the opportunity when you're talking on the phone or watching a movie.

It's wise to house your backups at another location outside your home office. I know one entrepreneur who sends her back-up disks to her husband's corporate office just for safe keeping. When working on book-length manuscripts, I've tucked mine away in my bank safe deposit box. Whatever works best for you will insure the safety of your important records, and save your sanity in case of loss.

Schedule an office-duties day

If you've worked at your own business for a while or researched a planned venture, you know a good portion of your time will be devoted to marketing your product or service, and then providing it. But when do you attend to the administrative details?

My advice is that you set aside an office-duties day. This could be once a week, a day every other week, one afternoon here or there— whatever works for you. During this time, make a point of filing papers, organizing or searching through existing files for needed material, sending out invoices, and tending the books.

Other times, particularly as you integrate work with raising the kids, you can squeeze in other necessary duties. Create a reading folder, and take it with you while you linger in doctor's waiting rooms or during swim practice and piano lessons. The home-based worker has to recondition the mind. Remember, you don't fit the typical mold. It's not like you can catch up on reading *The Wall Street Journal* during your morning commute. Make a list of what administrative or management tasks you need to handle, and brainstorm in another column how you might make time for these. Seize any and all work opportunities.

Working with your spouse

When it comes to teaming up with your spouse in a business venture, there are significant rewards and drawbacks. By reading future chapters, you might want to take a look at whether a partnership is the right kind of venture for you (Chapter 4) and how you can nurture yourself and your marriage (Chapter 10).

However, the most common rewards of working together include:

• Working toward a common goal.

• Increased empathy. No one knows the ups and downs of entrepreneurship better than a comrade in the trenches.

• Family flexibility to better meet everyone's needs.

• Increased opportunities for intimacy.

These benefits are tempered, though, with a few drawbacks.

• It's financially riskier to have all of your income tied to one source.

• Working together could lead to role conflict at work and in the marriage.

• The two of you might suffer from too much togetherness (and lack being refreshed at the end of the day with work stories).

• You could find yourselves in a power struggle (remember, a good marriage requires the ability to meet each other halfway on a lot of issues).

Every home-based business is different, so you'll need to judge for yourselves whether working together will be a strain or a success.

If you choose to pursue a business "marriage," it's wise to anticipate the problems raised here and discuss contingency plans if you do run into difficulties. For example, to avoid a power struggle, you both might designate one of you as "the boss." Or to minimize the financial risks, you might agree that one of you should maintain a part-time job.

How to switch mental gears

Think of your mind as a gear shift. One minute you're in "drive," helping your children with their homework or tucking them into bed. The next, it's a quick "reverse" into your home office to focus on business at hand.

It's harder than it seems, especially with children. If your daughter went to bed pouting because you read one story instead of two, you might still feel guilty, or even perturbed if you'd agreed on a one story limit.

If you have problems switching gears, try a few handy tactics. The first is a meeting of the minds. A meeting in *your* mind, to be more precise! Remind yourself that you have a job, it must be attended to, and that you'll tolerate no excuses, no procrastination. For me, I've made the most of nap times and occasional day care or preschool. As soon as the boys were safely in the crib, or off to school, I got to work. No exceptions.

Developing such a disciplined routine should help. So should rewards. Give yourself the promise of a well-deserved break, or a special treat if you achieve a particular goal. This treat could be as insignificant as a cup of tea or as elaborate as a weekend getaway, depending upon the circumstances.

Switching mental gears is also easier if you limit work to your office, and live in the rest of your home. That worked pretty well for me until I began using a laptop computer. Then I found I worked virtually anywhere!

Finally, if you find you're still having trouble making the mental shift, perhaps your goals aren't as compelling as they should be. Back to the meeting in your mind. Just like a novelist must establish the proper motivation for a character, you must have something that drives you. Whether it's inner satisfaction of a job well-done or the financial remuneration of your efforts, motivation sparks your fire to succeed.

Maintaining a positive mental attitude

Are you your own worst critic? Do you often see successful businesspeople or entrepreneurs and doubt whether you have the same fortitude to venture ahead?

Doubtful moments will surely be a part of launching your business. They might even last throughout much of your first year. During these times, tally your successes and remind yourself of them. In my first book, *Writing for Money,* I talk about building an "encouragement file," filled with complimentary letters, performance reviews from previous jobs, awards, copies of large checks, and other material that speaks loudly to my success.

Other ways to boost your mental attitude might include seeking out feedback from former co-workers, finding a mentor, and joining or creating a self-employed support group.

Try to determine why you feel insecure at times. Could it be that your mistakes overwhelm you? Maybe your family, former bosses, or peers fed you a steady diet of downward messages?

Even if previous transgressions haunt you, remind yourself that you can always become the person you want to be. Don't be idle. If circumstances have brought you down, change them and be in control of your life's destiny and career progress.

Building your own self-esteem can be a challenge, but if you weed out the "I should" and the "I can't" thoughts from your consciousness, you'll be headed on the right track. Robert Kennedy once said that some men see things as they are and ask why. He saw things that never were and asked why not. Ask yourself the same about life, and about your home-based career.

Rid yourself of rigid thinking. Surround yourself with the proper influences. Read inspirational books like *Success Through a Positive Mental Attitude* and *Think and Grow Rich* by Napoleon Hill and W. Clement Stone. In fact, there might still be a Page-A-Day calendar with contents similar to these books. For more tips on nurturing yourself and combating stress, turn to Chapter 10.

Resources

Start Up: An Entrepreneur's Guide to Launching and Managing a New Business by William J. Stolze (Career Press).

Start-Up Financing by William J. Stolze (Career Press).

The Small Business Troubleshooter by Roger Fritz (Career Press).

Partners at Work and at Home: How Couples Can Build a Successful Business Together Without Killing Each Other! by Annette O'Shea-Roche and Sieglinde Malmberg (Self-Counsel Press).

Honey, I Want To Start My Own Business by Azriela Jaffe (Harper Business).

Success Through a Positive Mental Attitude by Napoleon Hill and W. Clement Stone (Pocket Books).

Think and Grow Rich by Napoleon Hill (Fawcett).

101 Home Office Success Secrets by Lisa Kanarek (Career Press).

Heart at Work: Stories and Strategies for Building Self-Esteem and Reawakening the Soul at Work by Jack Canfield and Jacqueline Miller (McGraw Hill).

See also the Appendix for addresses, Web sites, and other information to help you launch your business.

Chapter 3

Carving out a workspace

Your home office may have been an afterthought. You made the decision to strike up a business venture—and turned the guest room, the basement, or even a corner of the family room into your workspace. Instead of setting up in an ergonomically designed workstation with everything efficiently and conveniently at your fingertips, you "made do" with existing furniture and available space.

No shame in that. Your office doesn't have to compete for coverage in *Architectural Digest*. It simply has to work for you and for your family. Other books may help you establish an office, but this chapter focuses on your office considerations as they affect your family.

Think of your office as a tool. Although it may not double your talent or triple your income, it will greatly improve your productivity. And rest assured, if designed correctly, it can affect your bottom line.

Start your search for the best-available arrangement by asking yourself some important questions:

- How do I like to work?
- Do I need a separate entrance for my home business?
- Do I need natural light or are windows unnecessary?
- Will my equipment need many power sources and electrical outlets?

- Will I need to establish room for potential employees?
- Do I need to install heating and cooling mechanisms in the space I select?
- Will I want to take a tax deduction for my home office?
- Have I chosen a space that's free of distractions?
- Is the office in a place where I can hear the kids and reach them quickly in an emergency?

It's possible that not all of these questions apply to your situation. If you have older children, no pets, or no spouse, noise and privacy probably won't be factors in your workspace decisions, so you could create a comfortable corner from any room. But if you have little tikes running around or income that's high enough to need that home office deduction, a corner won't cut it.

Location, location, location

The ideal space will have some degree of seclusion, accessibility, and security for your work (especially with little ones around). From the get-go, there are a few spots in your home you might want to steer clear of. The family room is one example. This room attracts the activity of others—television and videos for kids, socializing for teens. Their needs are very incompatible with yours as a home worker. Conflict is almost a given.

Of course there are exceptions to every rule. Because this book's focus is combining your career with your kids all under one roof, you may very well welcome a room arrangement that allows you to work on business projects while your children complete their homework assignments right next to you. So, truly, it's all in what works best for you and your family.

No matter who uses the space, there are other details requiring thought. There's temperature. The ideal range is 65° to 72° with humidity around 30 to 40 percent. Very hot conditions will literally fry computer equipment. And I learned the hard way that dampness does terrible things to your books and software, as well as your equipment.

Lighting and electrical conditions become factors for various tasks. Windows require shades or blinds to adjust light levels. Replace wall switches with dimmers to allow maximum control. Don't place your computer on the same circuit as your room air conditioner or any other appliance that cycles on and off (like a refrigerator) as power surges could ruin your equipment.

Always buy a surge protector for computers, printers and the like. *Consumer Reports* recommends purchasing a surge suppresser with a statement on the package verifying that it meets the "UL 1449 standard for TVSS."

You want to give yourself adequate space with a separate work surface for your computer and another one for writing and paperwork.

Finally, store disks away from telephones, vacuum cleaners, or other appliances that emit magnetic fields—you wouldn't want to risk having your disks erased. Computers, printers, answering machines, phones, fax machines, and other gadgetry should be kept away from sinks, food preparation, or eating surfaces.

Six ways to clear clutter

This subject could take several books alone to discuss, but it's important to mention because clutter comes between you, your work, and your family life. As you search for the ideal location for your home office, this might be the most appropriate impetus to have that garage sale. For many people, a day or two with sleeves rolled up, sorting through closets, attics and basements, yields not only added space but profit (not to mention a satisfying feeling of accomplishment). For those reasons, I recommend setting aside the time to purge. But how?

1. **Purge files periodically.** No doubt you'll find information you can use and forgot you had, but more than likely you'll fill a waste basket with excess you no longer need. Although my workdays are devoted primarily to work, there are times when there's a breaking news story I want to catch, or I deem listening to Dr. Laura Schlessinger's radio program a boost to my sanity. During those times I don't sit there idle, just viewing or listening. I gather my files and begin to sort.

2. **Begin clearing closets and other storage areas.** If you have a problem parting with material, look at it this way: There's probably a full ream of paper buried in your office that could be recycled. You'd be doing your part to save the environment.

3. **Uncover items that friends or family could put to good use**, or that you could sell and recoup some of the costs.

4. **Purge in spurts.** Part with what you can, a little at a time. Things become less sentimental over the years. Set aside a day, at least twice a year, to do spring sorting and pre-winter conditioning of the premises.

5. **Rationalize.** You've heard the clichés before, but a few are worth repeating. If you haven't used it in the last five years, chances are good you won't use it in the next five. When new items come in, old items go out. Whenever you purchase new clothing for yourself or outfit the kids each September, clear out what no longer fits. And giving is better than receiving. As a writer, it's hard for me to part with books and magazines. But if I can find it in the library, or unless it's absolutely vital to my professional existence to have my own copy, I should donate these books to others who don't have the collection I have.

6. **Move.** I'm not telling you to sell your house, although I believe if we all moved at least every 10 years, clearing clutter wouldn't even be a topic here. What I am suggesting is that you move things around. When Andy was 8 and Alex 3, I moved their bedrooms. That meant clearing out what was the guest room, sorting through Andy's clothes and toys (much of which could get passed along to Alex), and then moving Alex into more grown-up digs. Subsequently, we created a new playroom/guest room in what used to be the nursery. Not only did I uncover a wealth of material to donate, sell, or pass down the sibling chain, I also created a new site for existing toys.

How to convert almost any space to a workplace

Meander through your house with a creative eye open to several redesign possibilities. Sunset Publishing's *Ideas for Great Home Offices* (see Resource section) is a gem to help the brainstorming begin. This resource reveals how to transform just about any space into a workstation.

Closet industries

Maybe in your initial search, you dredged up a dozen boxes from your storage room or closet. If you haven't used anything from these boxes in the past six months, it's time for action. Rent an off-site storage locker for the load and convert the area into a viable workspace.

If the closet you've chosen is small, remove the doors to prevent claustrophobia or replace with accordion models. When not in use, the office disappears behind these folding doors, securing your belongings and hiding the clutter.

Some closet conversions span the length of one wall. Others allow you to build a desk surface right into the wall or to purchase specially designed computer furniture, with pieces that slide out for convenient use. Install recessed lights so that other fixtures don't take as much room. Halogen and fluorescent bulbs produce more light, last longer, and use less energy. Paint the walls a light color (such as off-white or a pastel) to make a small space feel much larger.

Utilizing your utility room

Storage rooms offer similar potential. Utility rooms can also accommodate a desk, chair, and a few files. The key to converting these small spaces is to use every inch of available space. Never place wall board over an area that could hold a couple of books or a few boxes of slides. Instead of trying to fit already-made furniture into such nooks and crannies, build a workstation on top of a pair of 28-inch file cabinets, and you won't even need to purchase a separate desk. Or install a drop-leaf, wall-mounted desk to save space.

Attic explorations

If you have some height to the attic ceiling, your home office could rise to lofty status. Run wood shelving around the angle of the walls. Build a ledge around the shelves and store decorative tins filled with your paper clips, pens and pencils, sticky notes, and other office supplies. If you position your writing surface directly underneath these ledges, you can also install fluorescent tubes to provide task lighting. Building surfaces into the wall or around filing cabinets saves space and money spent on unnecessary furniture. Make sure your attic is well-insulated to protect from the extremes of winter cold and summer heat.

A basement business

Many techniques already discussed will work in the basement as well, but there are special precautions down under. Chief among these is waterproofing. Paint the walls with a waterproof paint that contains a mildew retardant. Because most basements have concrete floors, you may want to build a subfloor over which you'll lay padding and carpet to further insulate. Carpet also adds decorative warmth. Partitions can hide HVAC units, water heaters, washers, and dryers. A drop ceiling hides ductwork, and insulation between the outside wall studs increases energy conservation.

Still no space...now what?

Many office supply and furniture stores now sell self-contained units that resemble a large entertainment unit on the outside. However, when you unlock and open the doors, therein lies your home office.

This handy, somewhat movable office provides everything but the chair you need to sit on. I say "somewhat movable" as you wouldn't be able to move it on a regular basis, but it could be housed in another room, at another time. It has shelf space above the computer work center and filing capacity below. To one side, there is a small desk area on which to write. There's even space for a telephone, answering machine, books and diskettes.

If these units aren't stylish enough for your decor, you could hire a craft worker to build a more elegant armoire to sit in your living or dining room. No one needs to know what lurks behind closed doors! If that doesn't work, purchase a decorative screen and hide a small workstation behind it.

Finding the right furniture

If money were your only consideration, there wouldn't be a problem with hand-me-down furniture or odds and ends from around the house. But it's not. You need a workstation that adds to your efficiency, not one that detracts from it. The right furniture for you depends upon the type of work you do. If you're like me and spend a good part of your worklife sitting in front of a computer, issues such as desk level and chair support are critical.

Select furniture that puts you at the right height. You can always raise a table by putting it on blocks, but too high a desk leads to poor body posture and causes arm, shoulder, and neck pain.

If you're a worker whose already suffered physical complaints—backaches, headaches, wrist or eye strain—seek out medical advice before remodeling or purchasing furniture. Watch out for the phrase "ergonomically correct." Some brands live up to that promise; others do not. I've known many keyboard-based workers with carpal tunnel syndrome and have discovered some symptoms in myself.

Another less important consideration is aesthetics. Few beyond yourself will view your office furniture, but if you expect clients or customers to stop by, you need pieces that look professional. A card table on wobbly legs may subtly suggest that your operation isn't so stable either. Even if no one else but you sees your setup, upgraded furniture might give you the added ego boost and sense of professionalism that help inspire you every day.

If you do need to purchase furniture, consider buying it used. Look for garage sales and flea markets, and going-out-of-business sales. One way to obtain furniture that's designed for office use is to watch the paper for notices of businesses that are relocating or closing. Often you'll find that they have excess furniture they'll sell to you for a great price.

Childproofing your office

When my oldest son was born, someone gave me a little plastic cup called a choke tester in which you'd insert items. If they fit inside, you had a safety problem—the item could cause choking to little ones. If you can't locate one of these in the safety aisle or in specialty catalogs, use the cardboard roll from a toilet paper roll. The circle is about the same size.

You'll find that many items in your home office present a hazard to your children. It's best to store these items in containers with hard-to-open lids, up high on a top shelf, or in a securely locked drawer:

- Paper clips, staples, rubber bands, erasers, brass fasteners, thumb tacks, push pins, magnets.

- Pens and pencils, scissors, hole punches, staplers.

- Glue, rubber cement, liquid eraser fluid, chemical sprays used for graphic arts or paste-ups, toner and ink cartridges.

Before you're satisfied your office is safe, get down on your hands and knees. If you were a curious toddler, what would intrigue you?

For instance, secure file cabinets and bookshelves to the wall with "L" brackets. Be careful what you throw in your office trash can, how your electrical cords hang from your furniture (or drapery cords hang from the window), and how the plugs fit into the outlets. In fact, purchase the closing devices that fit over the outlet or switch plates to minimize the temptation, and secure cords with window devices or cord holders (flex tubing).

When purchasing furniture and equipment, refrain from anything with sharp edges or glass surfaces or, at the very least, purchase corner-and-edge protectors. Opt for locks on desk drawers and file cabinets. Banish baby walkers from your office (and the rest of your home as pediatricians deem these devices unsafe).

This is all for your child's safety. But if you've spent money printing customized paper, stationery, envelopes and business cards, you'll want to keep these securely out of reach as well. We all know what a toddler can do with a magic marker!

Doorknob covers keep children out of closets and offices. When they reach the age that these don't deter them, your children will usually understand what's off-limits.

You may be able to do without some office supply items that you deem dangerous and not vital to your work. On the rare occasion I require a paper cutter, I use one at my office supply store to eliminate a serious hazard in my office.

One last word of advice. If space allows, set up a portable playpen or crib. Then when you do have paper clips, push pins or other items out on your desk, baby will be safe and you can complete your work.

Selling outside your home

For various reasons, your home might not be the appropriate outlet to sell arts, crafts, or other products. If you live in a high-rise or in certain residentially zoned neighborhoods, it's out of the question. You also might not want strangers coming to your home.

One easy idea is to rent a cart and the space it occupies in a mall or shopping center. If you can afford the actual space as well as the time commitment, you could use weekdays to create your crafts and weekends to display them as shoppers abound. If your budget is tight, limit the rental to peak weekends that attract crowds. Thanksgiving weekend and the weekends before Christmas, Valentine's Day, Easter and Mother's Day are your best bets.

If you wish to present your crafts in your home once or twice a year, you might try the approach my friend Donna takes. Every November, Donna invites several crafters to display their wares in her house. She takes out ads in local publications and posts signs. For one weekend, sheets cover her sofas displaying snowmen and stockings, peg boards hold ornaments and wreaths, and her kitchen becomes a gathering place to enjoy a cup of cider or coffee as well as a quick bite of lunch and dessert. Donna asks for 15 percent of the proceeds from the crafters she invites, and also uses this opportunity to display direct-marketed products she sells like Avon cosmetics and a line of health-care products.

Some churches and synagogues sponsor craft fairs where woodworkers, crafters, florists, and seamstresses rent tables or booths and display their work. Events like these generally attract larger crowds because some customers may be more comfortable coming to a large hall than a private home. Such bazaars or fairs are long-established traditions in many communities.

Finally, you might consider selling your work on consignment to other merchants who actually rent space and pay that kind of overhead. Sure you're giving them a cut of the profits, but then you eliminate the hassle of setting up and tearing down.

Do you *really* need a computer?

DOS? PC? RAM? CD-ROM? It's a foreign language to most of us who rely upon computers to accomplish our work, but don't exactly understand the intricacies of the technology. Not that you will walk away from this chapter as a newfound expert, but I hope to offer you the basics to aid you in the purchase of any equipment you need.

Chances are if you're a writer, designer, accountant or computer consultant, computers have become essential to your livelihood. But if you've never worked with a computer in the day-to-day execution of your job or trade, do you need one now? There's no easy answer to this question, but here are a few things to consider.

If you decide to telecommute, you will in all likelihood need to transmit files electronically, have an e-mail account, or use your computer's modem to fax information to co-workers or your boss. But also, a computer system allows any businessperson to track invoices and organize expenses, prepare for tax season, generate billing, keep copies of correspondence (including e-mail if you use this method of communication), generate estimates complete with charts and graphs, and create promotional material such as newsletters, news releases, and brochures. Even if you're computer illiterate, it's probably a good idea to join the information age and make the investment in technology. Once you do, you may wonder how you ever lived and worked without it. For the uninitiated, here are a few of the basics:

- *DOS* stands for *disk operating system*—the industry-wide IBM-compatible operating system standard—and essentially your computer's foundation software.

- The *microprocessor* is the computer's memory with information in temporary storage. Permanent data is stored in the *hard disk* (see below). The microprocessor is sometimes calls the *central processing unit (CPU)*, and its speed depends upon the microchips that make it work. That speed is measured in *megahertz (MHz*, or millions of cycles per second). The greater the *clock speed*, the more powerful the chip, and usually the higher the price.

- A *graphical user interface (GUI)* lets the computer user select pictures or *icons* to carry out commands, rather than type in commands and codes. GUI environments work best with a *mouse*, a small device that helps the user point and click on commands.

- *RAM* is short for *random-access memory*, or temporary storage. This is where the software programs you are currently working on are stored, but if you shut down your system or turn it off, all the information stored in RAM memory is forgotten and lost. RAM is measured in *megabytes (MB*, millions of bytes). It is usually offered as 2MB, 4MB, 8MB, 16MB and increasingly higher intervals. The larger the number, the more memory your computer has, and the better off you are.

- Your *hard disk drive* is a data storage device that's fixed inside your computer, faster and easier to retrieve from than a *floppy disk drive*. Hard drives are measured according to how many megabytes of information they can store. Again, the higher the number, the more storage capacity, and the more you'll pay. Get as much disk space as you can afford because a hard drive is very much like your closets: you can never have enough. Look for numbers like 500MB or more, all the way up to one *gigabyte* (one billion bytes) and beyond. Floppy disks come in two sizes—5.25 and 3.5 inches, the latter of which is now more common.

- A disk *cache* is included with the purchase of some computers, but it can be added later. The cache greatly enhances speed performance, so it is worth considering from the start.

- *Fax/modems* transfer information, and they're rated according to their transfer speed or *bits per second* (*bps*). Common bps speeds are 2400, 4800, 9600, 14400, and 28800. The higher the number, the higher the price (but the faster you'll work).

- *Multimedia systems* have become increasingly popular in the 90s. They're made up of a monitor, a system unit, and a keyboard, just like your computer. However, multimedia systems also have extra hardware that allows your computer to use enhanced sound, text, graphics, and video. Because they use *CD-ROM* disks, they're especially useful for educational, research, and entertainment purposes (see Chapter 8 for recommended products).

Shopping for computer equipment

Most computer equipment is nearly out-of-date the minute you remove it from the box. It's a losing battle to try to keep up with the latest technology. When you decide to purchase a computer, first and foremost, you need to determine your needs. Will the system support only your home business or will you allow the children to use it for schoolwork? Must it be compatible with the systems that your clients have? What kind of work will you do? What software will you run?

The answers to these questions will help you determine whether to purchase a IBM-compatible or Macintosh system. Although Apple introduced Macintoshes that are IBM-compatible, they are a little pricey. These answers also determine the amount of memory (RAM) and disk space (data storage) you will want. The central processing unit (CPU) dictates the speed. The higher the number, the faster the computer's response.

Read about the latest technology and the capabilities of the systems you're considering. Computer magazines such as *PC Magazine, Home Office Computing, MacUser, MacWorld,* and *Consumer Reports* will have the necessary comparative data. So will local computer user groups and Internet newsgroups.

Narrow your selection. If you need portability, consider buying a laptop model. If you only need word processing capability, a black and white monitor might suffice. On the other hand, if you plan to browse Web sites and install educational or game software, a color monitor is your best bet.

Just as you test-drive a car before you purchase, be prepared to sit down for an in-depth demo. Bring along a current project. Do you feel a sense of ease using the computer? How does the keyboard feel? Is the screen comfortable to your eyes? How will the computer system fit into the workspace you've created?

Seek the best price. Compare prices advertised in mail-order catalogs, computer stores, office supply outlets, and through dealer programs. If you are an educator you can purchase equipment at an educator's discount through Apple's Campus Direct program.

Be wary of used equipment, but don't totally rule it out. Your best bet is to buy from friends or relatives when you know the history of the equipment you're considering. If you purchase equipment from a stranger, write up an agreement that gives you several days to try out the equipment, with the ability to return it for full-price if it's found to be defective.

Consider the peripherals—scanners, modems, and printers. A *scanner* allows you to scan hard copy (printouts) and input the data into your system. However, if you would only use a scanner rarely, some copy centers have these available for your use.

An *external modem* sits alongside your computer and plugs into a spare serial port and the telephone jack. An *internal modem* is mounted inside your computer, connects to the wall jack for your phone, and is generally less expensive. High-speed modems are more expensive, but may save you time and telephone charges that accrue as you transfer data. The *fax/modem* allows you to fax to another party right from your computer and receive files in the same manner.

Printing prerequisites

Printers are distinguished according to their *dots per inch* (*dpi*) resolution. Some printers have a resolution of at least 300 dpi, compared with 1200 dpi of professional typesetting equipment. When examined closely, the 300 dpi print appears to have rough edges or "jaggies" on the characters. More dots per inch is desirable as it yields better resolution. For a typical home business, a resolution of 600 dpi is generally sufficient.

PostScript is a page description language, a programming system for the printer, developed by Adobe Systems. With PostScript, you can create type that looks a lot like what professional typesetters generate. The number of typefaces (more than 35) that come as standard equipment has made Post-Script popular. This selection of fonts, and the ability to make them virtually any size, gives desktop publishers great flexibility in the documents they can create.

PostScript also affects graphics. "Encapsulated" PostScript graphic files can be incorporated into many documents, scaled to any size, and printed on any PostScript printer. You pay more for a PostScript printer, but if your work demands a very high quality and variety of type, it's worth considering. In recent years, PostScript printers have been appearing at lower price levels.

Having your printer in the shop does limit the amount of work you can accomplish. However, it shouldn't shut down your business completely. When you decide to purchase an upgraded printer, you might consider hanging onto your old model as a spare, using it for drafts or emergencies.

If you don't have an extra printer sitting around, you might try faxing your work to clients or customers. Or with a fax/modem, send your material to a friend's computer and print it out from there.

Another option would be to take your laptop or diskette to a copy center that has compatible printers. Print out what you need, even if you're paying for the computer time. It sure beats not having any printer at all.

Seeking technical assistance

Most people are apprehensive when trying to set up fancy equipment with sophisticated features—particularly if that equipment has set them back a bundle of money.

If you need simple assistance on how to format a disk, set up a hard drive, connect a printer or modem, or get online, you might want to turn to a good reference book. Publishers have entire series of books on how to use various computers, software, and utilities. Next there's your local computer user's group or continuing education course. Computer classes tend to be very popular at community colleges and adult learning centers.

Keeping your computer clean

If you've spent money, time, and energy to purchase and learn to use a computer, it only makes sense to protect your investment. Here's a handy list of spring cleaning you can do any time of the year:

- Perhaps the best protection from the elements is to keep computers and printers covered when they aren't in use. Your local office supply store should have covers to fit your equipment.

- While dirt, ashes, or crumbs can damage a keyboard, so can cleaning fluid. A can of compressed air spray will gently remove grit from between the keys. Never try to pry off keyboard caps.

- Use a lint free cloth and glass cleaner to wipe a dirty monitor screen. Spray the cleaner on the cloth, then wipe down the screen. An antistatic screen cleaner can help if you need it, but before you use any product, check the manufacturer's guidelines.

- A mousepad comes with a washable surface, so if you don't already have one, it would be a wise purchase. A damp, lint-free dust rag wiped over the pad should be sufficient. Follow the guidelines for mouse care in your owner's manual. Mouse-cleaning kits are also helpful.

- To protect your equipment from the ravages of thunderstorms, be sure to unplug everything, along with your modem. Just as power surges can come in through your power lines, they can also enter via the telephone line. A surge protector helps, but it's worth taking the extra precautions.

"If you have purchased a brand new computer system, the seller should be able to provide assistance regarding how to hook it up and get it working, even if they do not come to your home," says Jennifer Boerio, vice president of communications for the Better Business Bureau of Western Pennsylvania.

If none of these options works for you, and you decide to hire computer consulting services, don't hesitate to call the Better Business Bureau to see if there have been problems reported with others using the company. Most consultants charge $30 to $75 per hour. "When consumers are looking for a professional service like this, longevity is certainly a factor to consider," Boerio says. "Not that we would discourage using any new business, but it lessens the likelihood that these people won't be around if there's a problem."

Selecting a cellular phone

It used to be that only the wealthy had cellular phones, but now with falling prices and competitive advertising, this technology, which was once considered a novelty, is becoming a staple of many small business owners. Determine your needs before you sign up for monthly service and equipment.

The majority of cell phone owners, according to *Consumer Reports,* have the convenience for safety's sake. Women especially like to know that they can call for help when stranded on a deserted highway. Next come professionals who want to stay in touch with their businesses before or after hours, frequently while sitting in traffic each day.

For the home-based businessperson, who works predominantly out of the home (that is, does not travel to client sites), and who confines business errands to a small radius, a cellular phone might be an unnecessary expense. Some users also find that there is a temptation to overuse their phone, and rack up expensive per-minute charges. In addition, carefully guard who has your number. Remember, you are paying not only for the calls you place, but for the calls you receive.

However, if you analyze your needs and set out to purchase a cell phone, try out a plan that doesn't require a long-term commitment, and one that carries no early termination penalty should you decide to opt out of the service. Beware of freebies: Introductory offers lure you with the promise of free air time or a free phone, but you're paying for these free items somewhere in your contract. And before you spend extra money for a nicer handset, remember that if you switch carriers there's no guarantee that phone will work with your new service.

Finally, use your mobile phone only for emergencies. Be sure that you can scale back your service at renewal time. And, protect yourself against cellular thieves who intercept your signal. Never give credit card or any other privileged information by way of cellular phone. In fact, if your provider can disable international service and you know you won't be needing that feature, then do disable it.

Saving the earth from your own office

Do you ever feel guilty for the paper you toss away in the trash? Or for the envelopes you tear open and dispose of? What about the supplies your office equipment consumes so rapidly? There are ways to be an environmentally sound businessperson. All the little things you do help to save the earth. Here are some valuable tips:

1. Use recycled paper available in spiral-bound notebooks as well as tractor-fed paper in your printer.

2. Use two sides of the paper whenever possible (for instance, I use the back side of manuscripts to feed through my old printer when I know I only need a draft copy).

3. Take your scrap paper to your printer who can cut it into smaller sheets and use adhesive to make small note pads.

4. Write with refillable pens rather than waste the plastic.

5. Donate old telephone directories, junk mail, catalogs, and newspapers to your community's recycling effort.

6. Cover up outdated return addresses on your envelopes with newly printed address labels (rather than toss the envelopes away).

7. Re-ink your typewriter or printer ribbons and refill toner cartridges for laser printers and copy machines.

8. Combine business errands so you're not wasting gasoline with little trips here and there.

9. Save those computer disks you get in the mail for trying online services, reformat them, and use these with a new label.

10. Turn off equipment, including fax machines and printers that aren't in use; print or fax your material all at once or in batches.

11. Don't mail something you can fax or send via modem or e-mail.

12. Use a small adhesive note that indicates "to," "from," and "date" when you fax rather than waste a full-size cover sheet.

13. Offer scrap paper to your budding-artist child who wants to create a masterpiece as you work nearby.

14. Turn folders inside out and relabel them.

15. Use ceramic mugs rather than Styrofoam cups for coffee.

16. Reuse packaging materials (including packing peanuts or plastic), carefully peeling off labels and adding your own (this means opening the package carefully in the first place).

17. Share magazines, newspapers, or trade publications with other at-home professionals, or donate them to your local library.

18. Ask larger businesses in your area what they plan on doing with their outdated directories or reference books, and if you're not a direct competitor, offer to take them off their hands when the new editions come in.

19. Show this list to your children, to other home-based workers, or environmentally-concerned friends.

Resources

Books

How to Streamline Your Life by Stephanie Culp (Writer's Digest Books).

How to Conquer Clutter by Stephanie Culp (Writer's Digest Books).

Conquering the Paper Pile-Up by Stephanie Culp (Writer's Digest Books).

Everything's Organized by Lisa Kanarek (Career Press).

Ideas for Great Home Offices by the Editors of Sunset Books (Sunset Publishing).

The Complete Home Office by Alvin Rosenbaum (Viking Studio Books).

The Home Office Book by Donna Paul (Artisan).

Home Safety Desk Reference by Dr. Ted Ferry (Career Press).

The Macintosh Bible (Peachpit Press).

IDG Dummies Series of books.

Magazines

Consumer Reports

PC Magazine

Home Office Computing

MacUser

MacWorld

Chapter 4

Starting small, building big

When I speak at conferences and answer listeners' questions on talk radio, I stress the importance of starting small. Grow too fast too soon and big disappointments may result. You could find yourself drowning under a sea of clients you can't possibly serve, or the increasing demands your empire wreaks upon family life, children, and your flexible schedule—the very reasons you sought work-at-home opportunities in the first place.

Brilliant dreams often color the minds of many who start out as self-employed workers. Writers automatically set their sights on the four-color, glossy magazines found on the newsstands. Consultants want to land contracts with Fortune 500 firms. And the average business owner can't wait to hand down some of the more tedious aspects of running a business to newly hired workers.

Throughout this chapter I'll emphasize the importance of slow growth as you establish your business, testing your concept in order to minimize unnecessary financial risk and emotional letdown. When you are comfortably handling the business and have the support staff (as well as family cooperation) in place, then you'll be ready to grow.

Continue your professional growth in personal terms by making networking contacts; purchasing related books and periodicals; investing in research and development; taking advantage of technology; and attending conferences and conventions. These opportunities usually come from minimal investment but lead to considerable rewards.

Loriann's top 10 home-business mistakes

1. Not doing enough research beforehand.
2. Passivity—if you're passive, your best bet is to work for someone else.
3. Poor time management.
4. Considering this to be less serious than a "traditional" job.
5. Not following the 80/20 philosophy—that 80 percent of your business comes from 20 percent of your client base. Keep these folks happy, for it's far less expensive and easier to market to current clients than to seek customers who don't have a clue who you are and what you do.
6. Not promoting your business frequently. Too often self-employed workers and small businesses look upon promotion as an unnecessary expense rather than the essential investment it truly is.
7. Spending too freely. As a friend of mine says, "You don't always need high-tech, just appropriate tech."
8. Not spending the money when called for—sometimes you will have to spend money to make money.
9. Not asking for help when you need it. Seek assistance—it's out there.
10. Not having a contingency plan to deal with tough economic times. Set yourself up to go without a paycheck for at least six months while you build your business.

Stay small for the short-term

Most of us think in terms of "How big must I be to...?" or "How much money do I need in order to...?" Few of us take the perspective of "How little money can I get by with?" or "How small can I stay?" But in the initial months, or even years, you will probably want to set limits on just how fast and how far you'll grow. Be realistic when you target your business's future: Few of us working from our homes have the space, resources, financial backing, and stamina to become a conglomerate overnight. In fact, just getting a business off the ground has probably caused a number of headaches.

For that reason, I suggest that you plan to stay small, at least for your first year. Gradually add a client or two or introduce a new product or service. Do it once you've established routines, developed a support system, have steady income, and are meeting client needs.

Staying small may mean turning down business from time to time. You could refer some business to your network of professional associates, or collaborate with someone who offers similar services. People appreciate a good plug, and what comes around goes around. Perhaps you could work out an agreement whereby you (or they) receive a finder's fee for the referral.

The client receives a needed service, your associate receives a referral, and you build goodwill and maintain the steady pace of your business without being snowed under.

Create a "board of directors"

If your growing business threatens to overwhelm you and your family, it may be time to seek outside expertise. A group of experts can give you more objective opinions when you're simply too close to the activities of your business. Properly chosen, this group represents years of experience and complements your own strengths. You might select from local business groups or trade associations, or use professionals such as attorneys, bankers, or CPAs.

An added benefit to developing a board of directors is the respect and comfort level that financiers (bankers, leasing companies, or venture capitalists) will have with your business. This is particularly vital when seeking further funds for your business's growth.

Because your company is probably not publicly owned, your board of directors will serve as an advisory panel to help evaluate your key decisions or strategies. You'll benefit from objective opinions and expertise, but you won't be bound by the recommendations offered.

Making a small business look larger

Although it may be in your best interests to stay small at first, that can be your secret. If you'd like the outside world and business community to view you with larger lenses, you can try these tactics:

- If you live in an apartment or condominium, you can use the word suite rather than apartment to describe your workplace and include in your address.
- If you go to mailing services, such as Mail Boxes Etc., you can rent an address as prestigious as you'd like.
- With the advent of voice mail, you can ask someone else to record your message that greets callers. This gives the impression that someone on your staff is answering calls.
- For correspondence, use the same approach, only with three lower case initials typed on each letter that departs your office. Some entrepreneurs use the initials "mbs" that stand for "make-believe secretary."
- Make strategic alliances with other professionals who can complement your work. For instance, if you are a writer, you can team up with a graphic designer for projects and list yourself "in partnership with," even if it is an informal working arrangement.
- List professional credentials or larger groups to which you belong. Knowing you belong to a nationwide community of your peers is very reassuring for some clients.

Networking your way to more business

I discuss promotion and marketing techniques at length in the next chapter, but be aware that one of the easiest yet most effective means of building your business in the early stages is networking. Personal and professional connections are invaluable whether you need a referral, an introduction, advice, or even moral support.

Make the most of existing connections. Remember the groups you belong to—professional societies, the chamber of commerce, the Rotary, or informal networking groups. Now is the time to call in those contacts and tell them all about your new endeavors. If you don't keep these businesspeople aware of your accomplishments, they can't possibly refer you to their contacts or offer you any referrals. Become a bit of an extrovert. If that's not your style, it's a goal for you to work on, for you must learn to interact with people, offering your knowledge and listening to theirs in order to grow, as a person and a professional.

If you feel that you need to add to your list (and who doesn't?), join some groups that meet in your community. Some of these meetings are listed in the newspaper. Ask friends or call your chamber of commerce for their recommendations. Try to include professional organizations, service organizations (such as the Lions Club or Kiwanis), and networking groups, to round out the types of contacts you make.

Bring a supply of business cards. Go to meetings prepared to stick out your hand, introduce yourself, and ask other business owners about their industries. Follow up accordingly. Chapter 5 deals with promotion in greater detail, but from the start of your business's inception, know that networking will make a difference and lead to greater success.

Hiring extra help in your home office

You're not alone if the prospect of bringing new employees (a.k.a., *strangers*) into your home office is a little scary. The reasons for this trepidation may vary. For some of us it may be for issues of security. Maybe it's the fear of dealing with the tax implications of being an employer. Often it's out of a sense that we aren't comfortable being the boss—avoiding personnel hassles may have been one of the reasons we left the corporate world in the first place. Yet none of these reasons justify not hiring someone if you really need the help. There are some ways, however, to get the help you need without having an on-site employee underfoot.

Hire an independent contractor

One option is to hire an independent contractor. Depending upon the nature of your business, this person could work out of his or her home also. Some job descriptions that lend themselves to this type of contracting include marketing, advertising, bookkeeping, collection calls, accounts payable and receivable, general business management, and record-keeping for tax purposes.

If you don't feel comfortable meeting your independent contractor at your home base occasionally, head to the local coffee shop. Set up weekly (or daily) meeting times. This approach gives you a direct line of communication and it gets you out of the house.

Today, with e-mail, faxes, modems, and telephones, you can align yourself with employees in other cities or states, and you might never have to meet face to face. In fact, if the person you hire works off-site, this is one test the IRS applies when determining employee status. It's a good idea to review these stipulations before you get yourself into a situation where you must withhold taxes and Social Security.

It's advisable that you inform whomever you hire, in writing, that he or she is hired on an "at will" basis. This gives you the right to end the employment at your discretion if things don't work out (assuming that there's no discrimination or other illegal reason for termination). Without such, it could be easy for the employee to state that the two of you had a verbal agreement for a specific period of time.

Hire an intern

A second hiring option is to farm out the work to knowledgeable people who need added opportunities to learn. Sometimes this is a very economical and thoroughly creative approach to your hiring dilemma. You can agree in writing to give course credit for an internship or independent study project to a college or graduate student. You'll have to offer some guidance and agree to supervise and evaluate the intern's work, but free help is hard to beat.

When I wanted to produce a Web page to promote my book *Writing for Money,* I knew I couldn't afford high-priced talent. A friend suggested that I search for a student. I called a former teacher who was quickly able to refer me to a current student—one who was quite interested in the Internet. I agreed to promote his talents and talk him up to my friends. In turn, he handed in my Web page as part of a class project. When that Web site was featured in a television segment, he was as thrilled as I was.

To start your search for an intern, approach the career planning and placement office or the on-campus internship coordinator of a college or university near you. Develop a job description and conduct interviews the same as you would for any other position. If you can afford some monetary compensation, this may attract additional candidates. If your budget is tight, stress the educational value the student will receive.

Hire family or friends

Working with a family member or friend can be done, and you *can* survive with your sanity intact. If you know someone within your circle who could help your business operate better, jump to Chapter 9.

Consider a partnership

It is possible you might be considering a partnership, and while it will certainly increase the manpower and perhaps startup capital, it also increases the complexity. If you are considering a partnership, get good legal advice before embarking.

Raising the cash you need

Try to avoid having to borrow a great deal of money. Begin with the most obvious sources—credit cards, family, friends, guaranteed loans. A good rule to follow is that you should borrow money for your business only to increase sales or decrease costs. Still, insufficient cash flow often necessitates the need to raise additional cash.

Whenever people first think of starting a business venture, they usually turn to the traditional sources of funding, which include personal savings, family, or friends to front the seed money. This may seem simple enough, but it's wise to keep such matters formal. Pick up a standard promissory note from a stationery store. Fill it out and have an attorney review it. Be careful when setting the interest rate, however. You don't want the IRS to consider the loan a gift and require the donor to pay gift tax.

If family and friends are reluctant to back your bright idea, ask them if they would guarantee a loan instead. And be willing to front some money yourself, usually out of personal savings. It's risky, but it's necessary.

Just as a bank rarely finances 100 percent of a new home's construction or purchase, it will be reluctant to loan you funds if you have not already pledged some personal savings. Look at this as you would a down payment. It demonstrates your commitment to the business concept. The drawback of using personal funds or those fronted by family or friends is that you put your nest egg as well as relationships at risk.

Other forms of financing include vendor credit and credit cards. In some industries, buyers have up to 30 days after billing to pay for any services rendered. Small business owners frequently use credit cards (especially those which offer frequent flyer points or other bonuses) to purchase supplies, equipment, airline tickets, hotel rooms, and other necessities. Credit cards offer convenience in the short term. Just be sure that this method of financing doesn't lead to long-term debt. Pay off any credit card balances as soon as possible. A good personal and business credit rating is essential to your long-term success.

Two additional avenues to pursue are customer/client financing and leasing. If you work in a business in which it's customary to purchase materials and pay other people while you're rendering your service, it's certainly acceptable to ask for a down payment. This helps you get underway and reduces the risk of nonpayment after you've delivered your product or service.

Leasing is a fast-growing method of attaining capital equipment. You gain immediate use of items without the expense of buying them outright. While there are tax advantages to depreciating equipment, through leasing you avoid tying up large amounts of money.

Finally, you can obtain financing through a bank or the Small Business Administration. You'll need a solid business plan and a good deal of persistence. You gain an edge when applying for a loan if you have helpful information already organized and ready to turn over to the bank. If it's an existing business, give a complete history. Personal resumes of principal partners and tax returns for anyone owning 20 percent or more of the business are needed.

Submit financial statements, including balance sheets and income statements for the past three years of existence. You should also submit a current interim financial statement for the period since the last fiscal year ended. Provide projections of your sales, expenses, and profit for at least one full year after you receive your loan. Your financiers want to see the expected consequences of the funds you borrow, so include these in your projections.

If a lender turns you down, ask why your application was rejected. Ask for a reevaluation after you've made any changes the banker suggests, and keep trying. Applying for a loan is sometimes a lengthy process. There may be additional paperwork and time spent, but the reward of further funds will be worth it.

Financial records

Cash flow is the lifeblood of your business at every stage, but especially when you're getting it off the ground. Seek a bank that gives you immediate access to your funds, preferably in your neighborhood, where you have developed a good reputation. If you must wait several days for deposits to clear, you could compound any cash flow issues.

It is certainly best if you have one account for business use and another for personal expenses. The same holds true with credit cards. Using one credit card solely for business expenditures eliminates the need to highlight, photocopy, and save selected portions of your personal credit card statement.

From the start, set up a habit of regular bookkeeping. As soon as payments come in, record and deposit them. Organize folders or files where you collect receipts. Depending upon your level of business activity, you'll want to review and organize these receipts often to determine your profit and loss.

I'll admit that when my second son came along and I had to trim some activity to care for his needs, I organized my receipts on a less-frequent basis. The cash flow (or lack thereof) didn't warrant the time each month. But I'd advise that you review your financial situation at least quarterly. Waiting until the end of the tax year to sit down with a box full of paperwork is daunting.

With the proliferation of software available today, it's easy to keep accurate records on your computer. This way, you won't overlook an all-important tax deduction, and you'll have the protection you need if your records are ever challenged by the IRS.

Insurance

Don't forget to protect capital investments, inventory, supplies, and equipment with adequate insurance. You don't want to have your laptop computer stolen from the trunk of your car only to realize that your homeowner's policy does not cover business-related equipment.

Add up the equipment in your home office. In many cases it will total several thousand dollars or more. Now check the exclusions on your current policy. If you're not adequately covered, you can remedy this with a business rider, or you may purchase a separate small business policy that would provide more extensive coverage.

Another type of insurance to consider includes computer insurance to protect against fire, theft, or the loss of data from a sudden power surge. This policy might even cover the temporary rental of equipment, should yours require repair.

Seeking legal solutions

From time to time, you might require more legal assistance than you can find flipping through the pages of even the best legal reference book. For instance, if you decide to establish a partnership, incorporate your business, fight a zoning ordinance, or trademark or copyright your work, a lawyer can help you through these and other processes. Just because your attorney drafted your wills or landed your neighbor a big malpractice settlement, doesn't mean this same attorney is the right legal adviser for your business.

Talk to other self-employed individuals or owners of small businesses and see who they use.

A good lawyer seeks simple solutions as opposed to costly litigation. The goal is to protect your interests while saving you money. If your attorney displays signs of the "fight and destroy" method, you can be sure you'll be spending considerable time in court and in front of your checkbook.

Ask in advance if you'll be charged for brief (10 minute) telephone advice, time not connected to your case, and inquiries about your bill. See if you or other qualified people such as paralegals on staff can do some of the legal research for less cost. If your attorney asks for a retainer, make sure any unused balance is refundable and get that in writing.

Valuable counsel considers long-term interests and tax ramifications of all actions. They refer you to other experts (namely accountants, magistrates, therapists, or others) for matters they aren't qualified to handle. Indeed, there are some matters you might be able to handle without high-priced counsel.

Disability insurance protects you if you cannot work for an extended period of time. What if you're diagnosed with chronic fatigue syndrome, ordered to bed during a difficult pregnancy, or suffer some other injury or illness? Home workers often don't make plans for these contingencies, deeming such payments unnecessary. If cost is a problem, look for protection with a longer period after the disability before the payments begin. This will lower the premium. If you insure yourself only to a certain age, such as 65, this could also reduce premiums.

Health insurance is also a significant part of the insurance equation. However, if you'll turn to Chapter 6, you'll find health insurance discussed in greater detail.

Collecting from slow payers

This chapter has dealt with the subject of cash flow, but no dilemma is more frustrating than facing up to the slow-paying customer or client. There are some steps you can take to ward off or solve a collections problem.

If you've required a down payment, you can be slightly more assured that the client will pay in full later. Why would they have paid anything if they were intent on being delinquent?

Send contracts prior to work and timely invoices upon its completion, with your payment terms stated very clearly. All you must include is a line to the effect that "Payment is required within 30 days of billing. Late charges beyond this date will apply."

Keep after slow payers. Establish a policy of prompt billing, follow-up notices, and phone calls. The longer you wait to collect, the more likely you are not to collect payment at all.

If you're working for a customer or client over an extended period of time, charge a retainer or make plans for installment payments. Lawyers do. Why shouldn't you?

As a last resort, turn over your uncollected fees to a collection service, or proceed in small claims court without the expense of attorneys, collection services, and such. Filing fees for small claims court are minimal (sometimes in the $25 to $40 range) and in most cases, a quick decision will be rendered. If you win, you may recoup court costs.

Find out if the dollar amount in question falls within the state's allowable limit (this is often several hundred to several thousand dollars). Check to see if you've exceeded the statute of limitations. If you're within a year of the billing, you're probably safe in proceeding. Do your homework. Spend a few hours in small claims court, which is open to the public. This will give you a feel for what to expect, and help you to know how to present your argument.

Ask yourself if you have a solid case. A good paper trail of written invoices sent and a phone log of collection calls made works to your benefit. So does a formal, written request for the payment delivered via return-receipt mail. Anything that must be signed for carries the message that you mean business, and sometimes this approach might work best of all.

Resources

The Smart Woman's Guide to Networking by Betsy Sheldon and Joyce Hadley (Career Press).

Start-Up Financing by William J. Stolze (Career Press).

Your First Business Plan by Joseph Covello and Brian Hazelgren (Sourcebooks).

The Ernst & Young Business Plan Guide by Eric S. Siegel, Brian R. Ford, and Jay M. Bornstein (Wiley).

Finding Money: The Small Business Guide to Financing by Kate Lister and Tom Harnish (Wiley).

The Business Words You Should Know by Brian Tarcy (Adams).

J.K. Lasser's Legal & Corporate Forms for the Small Business (Macmillan).

How to Run a Small Business by the J.K. Lasser Institute (McGraw Hill).

The Small Business Financial Resource Guide (National Small Business United).

155 Legal Do's (and Don'ts) for the Small Business by Paul Adams.

Inc. Yourself: How to Profit By Setting Up Your Own Corporation by Judith H. McQuown (Harper Business).

Government Giveaways for Entrepreneurs I, II, and *III* by Matthew Lesko (Information USA).

Chapter 5

Promoting your business

So now you've got your office set up, files in place, business cards printed, childcare arrangements figured out, computer plugged in. You're ready to roll, right? Not unless you have customers lined up! And you won't have clients calling if they don't know you're there. The phrase "Build it and they will come," is the stuff of great movie scripts, but not a reality for most new business owners.

One very important aspect of launching your new business is *marketing* your service or product to the people who are most likely to be interested in your business. Marketing means getting the word out about *you*. Marketing can be a complex and multifaceted process, and may involve a variety of efforts including advertising, direct mail, telemarketing, sales, publicity, public relations, research, and more. It's no wonder that most successful corporations support and invest significant resources in mighty marketing arms.

As you get your business off the ground, I can't overstate the importance of marketing to your success. The good news is, you don't have to have a marketing department, a complex plan, or even a hefty budget to promote yourself effectively. In this chapter, I suggest some inexpensive yet powerful strategies for getting the word out.

From the very start, the key factor in promoting your business is knowing exactly who your customers are. Big businesses may spend hundreds of thousands of dollars to gather this information—conducting surveys, setting up focus groups, gathering and analyzing data. You don't have to go to this extreme to get a good sense of your primary market.

Let's say you start a business to write resumes. Common sense tells you that your customer is someone who is looking for a job. Who might this be? In addition to employees unhappy with their jobs or whose companies are poised to downsize, a good market might be college students ready to graduate within the year.

Now that you've established this, your next step is to determine how best to reach these prospects. Your promotion strategies might include placing an ad in campus newspapers; posting flyers in student dorms; promoting an on-campus workshop on resume-writing; contacting professors and student counselors with information about your services; and asking for referrals.

Those strategies are a lot more targeted—and less-expensive—than creating and airing a TV commercial, and they're bound to bring better results, too.

Again, it's essential to identify your customer, your market. Once you've successfully done that, you can make decisions about how to reach them and promote your business. Here are just a few ideas to get you going.

Word of mouth: still the best form of advertising

You've heard it before, but word of mouth referrals remain one of the most effective—and inexpensive—means of promoting yourself. One glowing recommendation from a trusted friend speaks decibels louder than a 30-minute infomercial, a neon sign, and a dog-and-pony show combined.

"That sounds easy enough," you think. All you have to do is please your customer—and he or she will go spread the good news about your business. Well, that may be true, but there are several steps you can take to maximize the goodwill from your good service and to increase referrals.

- Ask your satisfied customers to tell their friends and family about you. Don't just assume—or *hope*—they will.

- Rather than leaving it up to your customers to spread the word, ask them for the names and phone numbers of others they believe could use your service. Then when you contact these people, be sure to mention whom they were referred by.

- If you receive praise, ask if you can use the comment, with a name, as a testimonial in printed literature.

- Ask your biggest supporters if they would be willing to serve as "satisfied customer" references. Often, uncertain prospective clients will request the names of other clients so they can ask them about their purchase experience.

- Reward your customers for referrals. If you put together and deliver gift baskets, and one of your regular customers refers you to a small business that starts to use you regularly, you might send the customer a thank-you basket, deliver her next basket for free, or offer an attractive discount on her next purchase or cash back for each referral she brings in.

- Consider rewarding the referrals, too. For instance, in the previous example, you might offer a five-percent discount, free delivery or, again, a small thank-you basket of their own. This has a double impact: It makes your *original* customer feel even more important—not only did she get rewarded for bringing you business, but her friends now know that she is a very influential person and she'll want even more people to discover this! And your new customers? They now know without a doubt that yours is the best gift-basket service around and they'll want to recommend it to others, too.

Powerful writing rules

Because writing is the foundation of business promotion, marketing, and communications, I thought it would be helpful to review a few writing basics.

- **Write in the active voice.** Active words allow readers to visualize what you mean. They cause people to take notice, believe you, and respond in the manner you would like them to. For instance, if I wrote: "Help is here when you need to attract attention to your work and alert the media," you would have some idea of my professional services. But if I substituted, "I will attract media attention for your work and increase your sales," you will have a much clearer picture of what I can do for you. And you'll be more willing to hire my services.

- **Weed out unnecessary words.** Spot the passive voice when you see forms of the verb "to be," as in "is, was, were," etc. Turn the sentence construction around. Get rid of clichés, including professional jargon that readers may not understand. If you can say something with a five-letter word rather than a 15-letter one, opt for the concise alternative.

- **Use the AIDA technique.** Copywriters keep their focus by remembering the mantra, "Attention, Interest, Desire, Action." This guides their work, and it should guide your written and spoken communication as well. Grab your customers' *attention*. Hold their *interest*. Instill a *desire* for the product you offer or the unique selling advantage of your service. And incite them to *action*. See how I tried to use this approach advertising a workshop I taught:

Attention—*Freelance Writing: Breaking Into Print.* So you want to be a writer and make money? Get started in six easy sessions beginning Tuesday, June 3rd.

Interest—Learn the basics of gathering ideas, writing like a journalist, and approaching magazines and newspapers on your way to getting published. Discover greeting-card writing, newsletters, commercial projects, even how to begin your own book.

Desire—Earn extra income as you turn a hobby into an exciting new career. Students will receive text as part of the course materials fee. For less than $50, you can start on the path to publishing, and even recoup your costs in your first sale.

Action—Space is limited, so register by calling 412-555-1234.

Finally, improve the style of your correspondence and speech. For this, you can use my book *Writing for Money,* or you can turn to the sage advice of Strunk & White in the classic, *The Elements of Style.* A quick review of this very concise reference will tighten and strengthen your promotions. I guarantee it.

How to write a news release

Often when I speak with people about marketing, they confuse the roles of public relations (or publicity) and advertising. Advertising is generally bought and paid for, while publicity is obtained for free. I bet *that* got your attention! But that's the point. Editorial coverage is far more powerful than advertising, not to mention much less expensive. In order to receive editorial coverage, however, you must know how to approach the media.

A news release is the standard tool used to announce your business, your product or service, or any significant news you want others to know about. It's the accepted correspondence that writers, editors and reporters receive. If your news release doesn't make these people take notice, it will likely be tossed aside, along with the opportunity to gain publicity for your growing company.

Make sure what you have to report in a news release is newsworthy in the first place. It might seem impressive to you, but to a seasoned reporter, it might be fairly mundane. Let the length of your news release announce the degree of importance.

For instance, if you are announcing the start-up of your entire operation, a one- or two-page release is warranted. If, however, you've recently won a new account, received an award, or plan to host a special event, a paragraph or two might well suffice.

Be concise. Journalists are trained to look for the vitals—the who, what, when, where, why, and how—in the lead paragraph. Start with what's most important, and stick to the facts. Adjectives and sales pitches belong in your sales literature, not in your news releases.

For truly insightful information, use quotations. Avoid all industry jargon. At the end, use a brief summary paragraph that states what your business is all about—in essence, your mission statement.

That covers the written aspects of the news release. Now for the presentation. In the upper left-hand corner of your letterhead, indicate "For immediate release." Across from that, in the right-hand corner, provide a contact and a phone number where you can be reached. Double-space the paragraphs of text, and at the end, use the "—30—" symbol to indicate you're finished. At the very bottom, flush left, you should include the date.

Address your envelopes to the appropriate editors, including their names, not their functions. Mail your release well in advance of the publication deadline. For instance, if you want to publicize a May seminar in a monthly periodical, you should get the news release off in February or early March.

Editors don't know what each news day will bring, so don't call to ask if your release will be used. Rest assured, if you've written it well, and if space or time permits, your release stands an excellent chance of being printed.

Consider sending your news release during routine "slow" periods. The time immediately following Thanksgiving and Christmas usually finds editors hungry for news.

Making friends with the media

Having your business featured or mentioned in a newspaper or magazine article or on a TV or radio segment is one of the best methods of promoting a small business or product. This *editorial* mention is perceived as more credible by the consumer than advertising, and it doesn't take huge sums of money. Unlike advertising, the media coverage you get is free. Your only investment is in the time and effort it takes to make good media contacts and keep them informed of events they might consider newsworthy.

In addition to regularly sending out news releases to targeted media, it's essential to develop and maintain good relationships with those professionals who determine whether your business is worthy of reporting. It's well worth the effort to identify the key media contacts and reliable freelance writers in your area.

Make an effort to identify those who will be most interested in your business and have the means to share your story. For instance, a seamstress should seek out those who write or report about fashion. A financial planner or insurance salesperson should target the business editor or consumer affairs reporter. A personal trainer or registered dietitian should send news releases and promotional material to the health correspondent. Don't forget to include the newsletter editors of organizations you belong to, or even the editor of your alma mater's magazine.

If you conduct business on a national level, rely upon directories such as *Bacon's Publicity Checker, Editor & Publisher International Year Book, Standard Rate & Data Service, Inc.*, and *Gale Directory of Publications and Broadcast Media*. Your library may have some of these resources. Otherwise, invest a morning or afternoon to develop a media list with names, phone and fax numbers, and addresses. Update your lists of editors, producers, reporters, and writers frequently.

Reporters will actually welcome your contact if it makes their job easier. In my town I've had great success promoting my first book. I know that the personal finance column of our major daily accepts material that fits the format. Several times I have faxed columns that were run as-is. I have studied the length and type of material that's needed for a television consumer affairs segment, and I've been interviewed multiple times.

When working with the media, meet deadlines, return phone calls promptly, be familiar with a reporter's beat, and know what story suggestions are appropriate to pitch. Be respectful of a reporter's time, and don't demand to see stories before they're printed. Once you have worked with a particular publication as a source, you may want to suggest a column idea to the editor. Don't limit yourself to consumer newspapers and magazines. Trade publications are less competitive, and sometimes easier to be published in.

Offer to send additional information, and if you really feel you have a newsworthy idea, ask for a brief meeting. Two T's are vital: Your information must be *timely* and *trendy*.

Mingling with the media is similar to networking in other aspects of your business. If a reporter is sent on a rush assignment, and she needs to think of a source fast, your persistence at keeping in touch and being helpful will pay off in additional publicity for your business.

The basics of advertising

For service providers, advertising is one of the costliest methods of promotion. It's good to understand how to capsulize your company message to create an effective ad—whether it's a classified searching for employees or a full-page, boxed ad in a community program.

Especially if you have a computer and some comfort level with basic desktop design, you should be able to put together some simple advertising yourself. Here are a few tips:

- The easier your services are to understand, the more effective the advertising will be.

- Use your business logo, any key phrases or tag lines that describe what you do, and make sure you provide a telephone number and/or address.

- Use your words sparingly and include plenty of white space in your ad's graphic presentation.

- Each word must sell, especially those you've chosen for your headline. Use active verbs.

- Negative expressions are word wasters. They detract rather than attract.

- Incorporating words such as "you" and "your" in your headline and ad copy speaks directly to your audience.

- Avoid exaggeration and jargon.

- When preparing ads for the yellow pages, realize that customers using these directories have already made up their minds to purchase your product or use your type of service. You don't have to give a sales pitch, but emphasize what is unique to your business. A phrase like "speedy service" belongs in your headline.

- For ads in the yellow pages or even newspaper classifieds, avoid using detailed photos or halftones, which may not reproduce well because of poor paper quality. Stick to simple line illustrations.

- Track your advertising. You'll want to know if one ad works better than another. Coupons work wonders this way. If you provide a mail-in response, use a department number or some type of code so that you know which magazine or newspaper the ad appeared in.

- Any artwork you include in your advertising must explain or demonstrate your product or service. Photographs work well when there is no substitute for the real thing.

- Borders and bullets attract the eye.
- Place your advertising when business is booming. Few realize that ads are most effective when a business is already running smoothly, for it takes time for advertising to achieve its full impact.

Direct mail

A direct-mail campaign can be extremely effective, particularly if you maintain an up-to-date database of clients and customers. Remember, there is no such thing as a former client, just a dormant one. So keep those lists current. I can't stress that enough.

In the event that you introduce new products or services, change addresses, run special offers, or announce achievements, these names will be very important to you. In my writing career, I've often kept a database of prior students and those who have written in response to my books. I can then send postcards alerting them to future books they might be interested in purchasing.

If you decide to use direct mail, there is a lot more to the process than I can confine to a few short paragraphs. There are entire books on the subject, but I will give you a few brief tips.

- Spend time developing your offer. How will it hook the reader? That enticement begins with the teaser, perhaps on the front of the postcard or envelope, which offers a benefit.
- Give enough information to answer any questions in the recipient's mind.
- The words you select must sell and the presentation should be neat, organized, and uncluttered. Using subheads, indentations, bullets, boldface type, and underlining can achieve this effect.
- Many direct-mail pitches contain a reply card, but unfortunately this card might be the only part of your package that is kept. Should this happen, you'll want all essential information to be on your card. Include details of the full offer, the main selling points, and instructions on how people can respond.

Selling yourself with newsletters

A good newsletter mailed out to customers and prospective customers can be perceived as a valuable resource, a mecca of important information, advice, tips, and news. Of course, for those of us generating the newsletter it serves as an effective promotional tool.

No matter what your business, service, or product, a newsletter can serve as a powerful means of communicating with your customers and prospects. If you're a financial planner, you can offer tips on how to choose mutual funds or stocks or reaffirm the need to save for the future. Real estate agents and interior designers can offer decorating and home improvement suggestions. A hairstylist could offer diet and nutrition information for healthier hair, plus coupons customers could use. With today's computers and desktop publishing software, it's easy to combine text and graphics onto a page (or several) that your printer can produce in mass.

The newsletter doesn't have to be several pages. Even a single sheet, front and back, might be enough to offer useful news to your readers—and get your name and service under their noses. Here are some suggestions as you consider spreading the word via newsletter:

- Choose a newsletter name that identifies its content. A good name helps position your newsletter, is easy to pronounce and remember.

- Self-employed consultants and professionals often use newsletters to enhance their professional images and to obtain media exposure. For this reason, consider using your name in the title.

- In terms of format, a three- or four-column approach yields the most professional look. A two-column approach is easier to read than a one-column format which looks like a typewritten letter.

- Format is the framework of your newsletter. It shouldn't change issue to issue.

- Collect samples of newsletters you think are good, and don't hesitate to use these for ideas.

- Use white space to avoid a crowded look. Boxes or tool lines, photographs, clip art, and pull quotes are all easy to achieve on a computer, and they attract the reader's eye.

- With graphics, more is less. As I say in *Writing for Money,* "Put a novice, with little graphics expertise, in front of a computer. Watch his eyes light up at the sight of bold-faced type, boxes, lines, and other elements. Give this person 50 different fonts, and he'll use them—all in the same document!"

- Think about mailing requirements. You can find more information about postal regulations and bulk mailings from your postmaster. Suffice to say, you can often save money with self-mailers because you eliminate the need for additional envelopes.

- Keep your content concise. Information should be practical—something the reader can use *as soon as he or she reads it.* Offer lists, numbered tips, and easy-to-follow, step-by-step instructions. Include fun facts.

- Don't forget your motive for offering a newsletter—to build business! Be sure to include a reason for the reader to do business with you (a discount on your service if the reader responds by a certain date, for example), and a means for getting in touch (a phone number or a response card).

- Hone your writing skills and become better equipped to work with clip art and photography. The skills will serve you well, not only in the creation of your newsletter, but in the general promotion of your business.

12 ways to toot your horn

Sometimes the best things in life are free—or pretty inexpensive. This includes promotion opportunities. There are plenty of creative ways you can attract attention to yourself and your business, establish your credibility, and have some fun as well. Here are 12 great ways to toot your own horn.

1. **Write a letter to the editor.** Comment on the business or industry you're involved in. Actually, letters to the editor receive a higher readership in many newspapers than staff-written editorials and syndicated opinion columns, so put your best thoughts into clear and concise form. Letters to the editor are not tirades. They state opinions, provide supporting facts, and suggest action. They always conclude with your signature, title, and name of your business.

2. **Sponsor a community sports team.** This usually involves little more than paying for team T-shirts—which prominently feature the name of your business on the back. Whether it's a men's basketball team or Little League, team sponsorship can offer lots of exposure—as well as additional business contacts from players or parents.

3. **Join a community service organization.** Although the focus of activity is on supporting the community or other worthy causes through fund-raising activity, most organizations (Rotary and Lions Club, for example) schedule weekly or monthly meetings. Often these afford an opportunity for members to speak about their business. Of course, the networking contacts and business referrals are valuable, too.

4. **Get on the board of a nonprofit organization.** Here's a great opportunity to volunteer for a cause you believe in and showcase your talents. Typically you'll find other influential businesspeople on these boards.

5. **Exercise your vocal cords.** No matter where you live there must be a place for you to speak out and offer advice. Let your willingness to speak in public be known to local men's and women's groups, the Rotary, the chamber of commerce, business and professional associations, even your child's school. If you listen to insightful talk shows, don't be afraid to call up and render your opinion. Informed callers are as necessary as the expert guests.

6. **Circulate your clipping file.** Send copies of articles you've been quoted in to other reporters whose work you admire. Also drop a copy of your newsletter in the mail to selected sources.

7. **Teach a class.** Perhaps through a community college, you could offer a semester of lessons in your area of expertise. Not only is your business exposed to a classroom of potential customers, you might get paid to teach. There are other opportunities, mostly voluntary, to teach: through the public library, at your local bookstore, through community organizations—you might even advertise a one-day workshop and hold it in your home.

8. **Sign up for career day.** Talk to high school students about your profession. In addition to imparting valuable experience and enthusiasm about your career to your future associates, you'll be making important connections within the school administration and—perhaps—getting some free media exposure. (This sort of event almost always gets a lot of play in neighborhood papers.)

9. **Remember your clients at special times.** Now that *you* are a business, you'll want to consider the value of giving gifts to your valued clients at holiday time. But perhaps even more valuable are opportunities to remember customers at other times. A card from you and your business acknowledging a birthday, a birth in the family, or an anniversary—even the anniversary of their first doing business with you—may have more impact than a cheese tray at Christmas.

10. **Maximize your charitable giving.** Contribute to your favorite causes in the name of your business. Often there are special corporate giving opportunities that buy you a little publicity, too. For instance, if you donate to a public radio station during their fund-raising drive, you can get air time. If you contribute to the renovation of an historic building, you may get a brick with your business name.

11. **Offer some freebies that offer *you* extra mileage.** Your clients will appreciate giveaways such as coffee mugs, car cups, hefty refrigerator magnets, pens, notepads, calendars, etc. The bonus to you is that your business name, address, and number are on these items and in front of your customer and potential customers as well.

12. **Entertain.** Those who display their generosity by buying someone else a cup of coffee, taking a client out to lunch, or hosting a dinner party or open house are usually remembered for these gestures. When I hosted a book party as a newly published author, a friend who works as a party planner helped me. It made a considerable difference in terms of my image and the enjoyment my guests had.

Targeting television talk shows

There's nothing like a talk-show appearance to draw attention to your product or service. One appearance on Oprah, or even your local equivalent, can boost profits considerably. And it doesn't cost you a penny for the publicity.

To gain the attention of producers and hosts, address a one-page letter to the program's producer, suggesting a specific angle for a segment and telling of your availability. Mention any appearances you have completed.

Supply a background that answers: "Why should I book this guest?" Provide any news clippings you have on hand dealing with the subject or any publicity you've received. Also offer sample questions. Follow up with a brief phone call two weeks later if you haven't received a response, being prepared to pitch the idea verbally if necessary. Should the producer like your idea and book you as a guest, ask for confirmation in writing and by phone, closer to the actual taping.

You aren't alone if you feel a little bit nervous about appearing on TV, but put it into perspective: If you are interviewed for a TV news spot, whatever you have to say will most likely be broken down into 30-second soundbites. If you're the guest of an hour-long call-in show, the actual time you'll be on air, after accounting for intros and commercial breaks, the host's remarks, and the guest callers, will be about half that time.

There are some steps to take that will boost your self-confidence and help your appearance to be a smashing success. Watch or listen to the talk show beforehand to become familiar with its format, audience interaction, and ratings appeal.

Think ahead about questions that might be asked and prepare some responses. Plan to dress appropriately, avoiding patterns that appear to be busy on camera. As a rule, solid colors are best. White appears too washed out on camera while black conveys a harshness and shows no detail. Red ties look good on men. Noisy or flashy jewelry is taboo for women.

Posture, mannerisms, and speech habits all help to convey an image. Talk to the camera and audience, not your host. Don't fold your arms across your chest or you'll look stiff and uncomfortable. Lean forward a little to show your interest.

In television, makeup is for everyone, including men. It eliminates glaring shine on the skin and avoids the washed-out look brought about by the intense lights. While some stations provide make-up assistance, others do not. Ask for a glass of water to sip during breaks or when your voice gets dry.

The benefits of videos and infomercials

Once you have a successful product or service, developing a video or infomercial might make sense for your marketing effort. Video production is costly, so you must weigh the costs against the profit potential.

Listen to what your customers or clients want. A friend of mine, Jan Larkey, worked as a color consultant who went on to pinpoint figure and fashion problems. "My clients started asking for copies of the illustrated sheets I developed. Light bulb! Why not mass produce and sell them to use for their own classes?" she says.

Jan then produced a training video. She listened to her audience, and when she attended national image and sewing conventions, she earned money as a speaker and from the sale of these complete training kits. "Sales poured in," she says. "Hundreds of training kits helped others expand their home-based businesses." Still listening closely, Jan learned that the charts were more difficult to use than a book would be. She ended up turning her efforts into *Flatter Your Figure,* which went on to sell more than 225,000 copies.

In another case, the late author Gary Provost taught a very popular New England writing workshop. Gary was in demand as a speaker at writer's conferences as well. But what about all those folks who couldn't afford the trip to New England, yet wanted to learn his approach to novel writing? Full-page advertisements for Provost's videotapes were frequently found in national writing magazines and he sold them at conferences.

You can spot other noted speakers and experts with their half-hour infomercials, which run late at night on many channels. Their marketing approach is usually designed to urge you to buy a book, an audio tape series, or additional videos.

Before you venture into producing an infomercial, read up on the subject. Investigate the companies that produce these. See if there are local video production firms trained to handle infomercials. And, remember, not only will you pay for the cost of producing the video, but there is the added cost of the media buy, which can be substantial.

Selling yourself on the Internet

Today, millions of people around the globe have access to the Internet, allowing them to exchange information, send mail, or transfer files. Access is available through online services (such as CompuServe or America Online), through corporate or educational networks, or via local Internet providers, which generally charge a flat fee for unlimited access to the Internet and the World Wide Web.

If you think using the Internet is too complex, expensive, or otherwise inappropriate for a home-based business, think again. It's not as daunting as it seems, and you can reap many rewards from having a presence online. Here are some simple ways to navigate the net:

- Establish an e-mail account. If you own a computer, you've probably received your share of free disks to try the major services. Use your free time to see what it's like at virtually no investment. If you decide to stick with the service, be sure to include your e-mail address on all business material such as your business cards, letterhead, brochures, advertising, and your e-mail signatures.

- Take advantage of the information exchange in newsgroups. For virtually any industry you're involved in, there's a group of people who routinely post questions and follow up with answers. You can offer your insights and post your opinions to various groups, and allow your signature file to identify you as president of a company, author of a particular book, etc. Just be careful with your "Netiquette." The pool of Internet users is usually well-educated and doesn't take kindly to blatant advertising messages. (In net jargon, they refer to this as "spam.")

- Develop a home page or Web site. Visit sites of other companies you admire and make a list of the features you like about them. A few pointers to consider:

  Concentrate on the text in your pages, not necessarily the graphics. Not everyone has the patience (not to mention the modem speed) to download dozens of graphics. The lure of the Web is the information it offers. Make your home page as interactive as possible. Quizzes and surveys get people involved. At the very least, you want folks to be able to send you e-mail. And your Web site should ideally give them other ways of contacting you through postal mail, telephone, or fax. For products, give simple steps on how to order. Build in links to other Web pages you recommend.

Hire a professional designer, seek out a student to assist you, or perhaps take a class yourself. But do make a point of learning about the Internet and the World Wide Web. Consider using search engines to spread the word of your site. Then alert the media to your presence as you announce your home page in a news release.

Calming sales-call phobia

It's perfectly natural to dread making the sales call, even if you have the advantage of a referral from a friend or fellow associate.

At one point or another, most self-employed workers feel much like the job seeker—always on the ask. Try to reframe the perception you have of this task. You have a skill and talent. Others may not know about it, or if they are aware, they probably could stand to be better educated—by you!

The best time to make sales calls, whether by phone or in person, is immediately following a success you've had or when you've achieved a stated goal. The enthusiasm will come through in your voice. The worst time is after you've suffered an ounce of rejection, feel ill, or are exceptionally tired.

Displace the fear and forge ahead. Make a list of key factors that you know set you apart from your competition. If you need to, keep this list handy. Keep the initial contact short to show that you value their time.

Offer ideas on how to improve your prospect's business. We journalists call this the service orientation, for if you can make someone else healthier, wealthier, wiser, more popular, or well-thought of, you have almost guaranteed an audience.

The best way to get rid of the phone-call fear is to do this on a routine basis. You'll win some. You'll lose some. Studies point out that for every purchase decision consumers make, they needed an average of four or five, sometimes as high as 10 or 12, mentions of you or your product or service before they acted. Take the time to convince your prospects. It will pay off. And you'll end up a more confident salesperson in the process.

Resources

Writing for Money by Loriann Hoff Oberlin (Writer's Digest Books).

Words That Sell by Richard Bayan (Contemporary Books).

Guerrilla Marketing for the Home-Based Business by Jay Levinson and Seth Godin (Houghton Mifflin Co.).

Guerrilla Marketing: Secrets for Making Big Profits from Small Business by Jay Conrad Levinson (Houghton Mifflin Co.).

Marketing Your Services by Rick Crandall, Ph.D. (Contemporary Books).

The 22 Immutable Laws of Marketing by Al Ries and Jack Trout (Harper Business).

The Nordstrom Way by Robert Spector and Patrick D. McCarthy (Wiley).

Making More Money On the Internet by Alfred and Emily Glossbrenner (McGraw-Hill).

Guerrilla Web Strategies by Vince Gelormine (Coriolis Group).

Electronic Selling: 23 Steps to E-Selling Profits by Brian Jamison, Josh Gold, and Warren Jamison (McGraw Hill).

InfoQuick, Guide to Infomercials by Dick Bruno (The Hawksbill Company).

The Infomercial Producer Report (American Television Time).

The Complete Guide to Infomercial Marketing by Tim Hawthorne (NTC Publishing).

Bacon's Publicity Checker & Bacon's Radio/TV Directory (Bacon's Publishing Company).

Chase's Calendar of Events (Contemporary Books).

Celebrate Today! by John Kremer (Prima).

Speak and Grow Rich by Dottie and Lilly Walters (Prentice Hall).

Six Steps to Free Publicity by Marcia Yudkin (Plume Books).

66 Ways to Make You or Your Business Newsworthy, by Marcia Yudkin (available direct for $2 plus SASE to Marcia Yudkin, P.O. Box 1310, Boston, MA 02117).

Chapter 6

Time- and money-saving tactics

No doubt, one of the biggest draws to home employment for the working parent is the opportunity to spend more time with family. Those who seek this benefit are often willing to risk a reduction in income for the priceless commodity of time with their children—only to find themselves in a dismaying dilemma: To make up for lost income, they must work harder, and by focusing more on work, they discover themselves suffering from the same time famine that afflicted them in the corporate world. This chapter will address time-saving techniques and cost-cutting issues, with the hope of offering you more balance in your work-at-home situation.

Dealing with distractions

It would be easy for me to suggest such time-saving strategies as "maintain regular work hours," "treat your job as you would at any office," "close your office door," and the like. These ideas are all valid. But they've been stated so often they seem like clichés.

If you don't let things pile up, if you undertake tasks as part of your periodic work routine, it's easier to focus when you need to concentrate on work-related tasks.

But if the dishes are clearly bothering you, or the dust is so noticeable you can't stand it, take a 20-minute break. Set a timer. With dish soap or dustcloth in hand, tackle as much clearing and cleaning as you can. Then, get back to work with the knowledge that you've put a large dent in, or perhaps even accomplished, what stood in the way.

When spouses or children could easily interrupt, make it clear what is an acceptable interruption. My sons have learned that if they are playing in the yard with one door to the house open and unlocked, they're to use that door to enter and exit. Unless they're bleeding or badly injured, I will not jump up every time they want in the front door if the basement is accessible.

Another way to cut down on interruptions is to make a game out of it. Play "stoplight," by having your children cut circles from colored construction paper. You will have three lights to use as signals: red when you have a pressing matter that means no interruptions (short of the house catching fire!); yellow to signal that they should proceed with caution (knock on your office door and enter if they must); and green, when you're doing light work and wouldn't mind some company or an occasional question.

Summer will almost certainly test these limits. It's worth repeating to your children that you expect certain courtesies throughout the day. Such things as entering the house quietly without slamming doors, limiting the volume of the television or stereo, and keeping playtime to a dull roar are all essential.

The same tactics work with neighbors or family members who call when you're sitting down to work. Instead of leaving them feeling rejected, try saying yes on your terms. Yes, you can help get that heavy box out of the car when you're finished at five. Or you'd be happy to sit and catch up over a glass of iced tea, but after dinner when you can each sit outside and watch the kids play. Too often our kids and others look upon home workers as being "bossless," but we have deadlines, and just about every home-based professional I know is responsible for making someone else happy with their work.

Finally, the kitchen calls your name if you're not careful. Indeed many home workers complain of weight gain. Dietitians report that these people must not overlook a nutritious lunch. Rather than go out of doors or off to a restaurant, simply go to your kitchen, and eat something healthy. Otherwise, the little trips to grab a handful of cereal or a bag of microwave popcorn will add up, put on pounds, and no doubt influence your work.

Keeping up with housework

My advice? Enlist help. Unless your children are infants or toddlers, and your spouse is incapacitated, get the family to pitch in (see the following section on children's chores). If this isn't an option, hire a professional cleaning service.

"What?" You object, "You expect me to spend premium dollars on housecleaning?" Hiring help really *does* make financial sense. Here's how: Let's say it takes you four concentrated hours to totally clean your house. If you bill your time to clients at $50 an hour, that's $200 of time that you're giving up for housework. Trust me, it won't cost you $200 to have a typical home cleaned. An individual may charge $40 or $50 ($10 an hour is the typical rate where I live) or a cleaning service might ask for $80 or so.

However, there are times when you'll tackle these tasks on your own. You can try a few tactics that make managing the household a bit easier.

- Make it a habit to clean up messes as they occur. Putting them off only makes them harder and more frustrating when the task faces you.

- Take inventory at the end of the day. Ask everyone to pick up their own belongings from the home's central areas. Straightening up before you go to sleep means waking up to an organized home and a better mood the next morning.

- For the sake of appearances (when visitors or clients make surprise visits), make sure your visible rooms have someplace to hide clutter. In the family room, it may be a big toy box, in the living room or office, it may be a large basket or an attractive trunk that doubles as a coffee table. When guests drop by, you can pick up toys, clothes, dishes, papers, books, and stash them out of sight before you get to the door.

- Keep a small plastic bucket of cleaning supplies in each part of the house, or underneath the vanities in bathrooms. When you need to clean up the sink or wipe the fixtures, you can take care of it when the urge strikes.

- Use synthetic-turf doormats to keep the dirt down, or simply ask people to remove their shoes upon entering your house (especially in inclement weather).

- Hand-held vacuums are great for cleaning crumbs, loose hair, dust, even drink spills.

- Put off major cleaning until late in the fall, after the last of the sand, dirt, and bugs have been tracked indoors. In the spring, tackle baseboards, windows, and outdoor siding that may have gotten grimy during the winter months.

- Reconsider your decor. You may love the look of Victorian clutter—lots of tables covered with knickknacks, figurines, and photos displayed on every available surface, pillows covering the chairs and couch, but it's just more stuff to clean and keep straight.

- Make it a habit to periodically go through old clothing, toys, books, and records. Donate, give away, or sell at a yard sale those things you no longer need or use.

- Determine which cleaning tasks you loathe and which you don't mind doing. If the budget allows, consider contracting out such things as window washing or carpet cleaning.

Chores children can do

Parents often wonder what their children can do to help with household tasks, without asking too much of them at any given age. There are numerous chores kids can help with, and build their own skills and self-esteem in the process.

The key is communicating exactly what needs to be done and walking the child through the task the first time around. Of course, every situation, household, and child is different, but the following suggestions might work with a little training, patience, and praise:

Children ages 3 to 6 can:

- Clear the table and load the dishwasher.
- Carry the laundry basket and put their items away.
- Help wash the car, or even the dog.
- Bring in the newspaper or mail.

- Pull weeds in the yard.
- Water outdoor plants.
- Put away toys.
- Set the table.
- Take the garbage to the curb.
- Squirt nontoxic cleaner on furniture and dust with rag.

Children ages 7 to 10 can:

- Do any of the chores above.
- Wash and dry dishes.
- Do simple yardwork such as raking or shoveling small amounts of snow.
- Prepare some foods.

- Feed pets.
- Unload the dishwasher.
- Dust and vacuum.
- Carry groceries from the car.
- Water indoor plants.

Children ages 10 to 12 can:

- Prepare portions of a meal or a simple meal in itself.
- Do yardwork not involving dangerous equipment.

- Wash the car on their own.
- Baby-sit younger brothers and sisters (provided you are within access).

Children ages 12 to 14 can:

- Mow the lawn.
- Baby-sit younger brothers and sisters while you run brief errands.

- Prepare meals.
- Use hedge and weed trimmers.

The parents I've talked with who have assigned chores to their children tell me they do so on a regular basis. They start with simple chores, and build to the more complex. For younger children, there's usually the reinforcement of a chore chart or list displayed on the refrigerator, or some other central location. Some parents even draw up an agreement with their children, agreeing to particular household tasks they can do. Everyone signs it so there are no misunderstandings later.

Views on whether to pay children an allowance are mixed. Some parents feel this diminishes the child's sense of responsibility, conveying that you only do work when there is monetary compensation involved. You might, however, decide on something other than money to reward your children for their help. This could be an added extra like a trip to the movies or choice of favorite restaurant.

"Someone help me, please!"

No one likes to ask for help, and some of us are less communicative than others. If you feel you're falling into the habit of nagging, begging, or pleading, just admit it. No one can fault you for honesty. At least you've made your needs known, which is significantly better than keeping them inside and acting out in a passive-aggressive or angry way.

Tell your children or your spouse that you do not mean to nag, but you truly would appreciate help. Ask them what they'd like to do to lighten the load. Negotiate your standards a little bit. And be willing to let your helpers learn their household skills.

If, after you've offered up your most heartfelt plea, a spouse or child replies, "Well, you're just better at doing this than I am," then tell him or her that you're very willing to allow for the learning curve. After all, most spouses are happy to accept the economic benefits of a working husband or wife—kids, too.

However, if you find that, despite your best efforts, essential tasks are still forgotten and your family remains reluctant to help, you need to talk about it. Keep the lines of communication open, and don't wait until you're exhausted beyond belief.

Meal-planning made easy

The first thing to do is find out what everyone's menu preferences are. Sometimes family members can remind you that you haven't prepared a favorite dish in awhile, and maybe they might get a thrill out of preparing it themselves.

My personal favorite meal-planning strategy is to cook ahead. Sometimes, I'm simply in the mood to do something with immediate results (as opposed to the delayed rewards of writing). So I take to the kitchen and get out the food processor and the crock pot. I find I can prepare several meals ahead in a short period of time.

While chopping things, I can grate frozen buns or bread for bread crumbs, cut up carrots and onions for soup or to have on hand. A large batch of ground meat might be the basis of that night's meal, but also provide mini-meatballs for the soup, or larger ones for next week's spaghetti. If I'm making one potato casserole, I may as well make two, freezing the second for a quick warm-up later.

Sometimes I don't have the components of an entire meal, but just having an entree that can be paired later with a salad or frozen vegetables is a tremendous time-saver. Try to freeze casseroles or containers that can go directly from the freezer to the oven or microwave.

If you don't already have a stand-alone freezer, I'd strongly suggest you purchase one. You'll find that thawing and reheating foods you've already prepared is not only convenient, but terribly economical when you consider the alternatives of take-out fare and restaurant meals.

Simplifying holiday hassles

Holidays are hectic, even without a home-based business. But *with* one you now have client gifts to buy, cards to send, and parties to go to. Why not ask all family members to make a list of their favorite holiday activities, and find out who else might be willing to help?

For instance, if one of your children enjoys baking cookies, or decorating the house, perhaps you can pass along these chores without feeling even the least bit guilty. This also avoids someone feeling disappointed because their favorite dessert wasn't made or some other tradition followed.

For the month of December, make mealtime less complicated by preparing casseroles or large crock pots that yield plenty of leftovers for the next night. If you need to accomplish baking projects on your own, make a list of the ingredients ahead of time and set aside one day to tackle this.

The same goes for gift shopping and wrapping. In fact, never go into a store without some sort of list to guide your purchases (and an address book if you must ship out of town). Try selecting a theme for adults gifts, as in giving everyone books, calendars, or CDs that can easily be purchased at a book superstore. Your theme could be sports paraphernalia or kitchen gadgets, just to make it easy on yourself to do one-stop shopping. Better yet, decide among close friends and family that you'll draw names, or give family gifts rather than dozens of individual packages.

Ask about free gift wrap or if that's not possible, designate a time when you can wrap on your own. Always plan for a few last-minute gifts. Stock up on generic items like mugs, picture frames, coffees, or teas, that you can give to an unexpected guest.

What about remembering clients with cards and gifts? I'd advise keeping that simple. If you want to have a special holiday greeting card designed or do it yourself with desktop publishing, start early in the fall. Your printer will love you for it! Sometime in November before the real holiday rush begins, get in the spirit and go through your Rolodex to make sure you don't miss important clients when addressing envelopes.

When I've sent business gifts, I've always sent the same thing each year, but I believe it's a gift that everyone has appreciated. Rum balls! I get out the Caribbean rum and set aside a day to make rum balls for family, friends and business associates. I package these in decorative plastic bags, tins or mugs, and send them through the mail in early December. Indeed, some clients count on their arrival each year, sniffing each package as it comes in the door (that's what they tell me, anyway).

Choose whatever type of gift you feel is appropriate, affordable, and manageable. I think gourmet or specialty food gifts work well because people aren't likely to buy them for themselves. When they get them, they're a real treat, and one they can share with family and friends, clients, or colleagues.

Your gift-giving could also extend to charities. For example, I serve as a member of the East Suburban Task Force Against Domestic Abuse/Violence. I know that the cofounders of this organization have their own medical billing and accounting company. I'm guessing that they'd be thrilled with a donation to the task force that's trying to raise funds for a safe house in our community.

Time-saving strategies

No matter if it's personal or professional time we're trying to preserve, time-saving tips net us more time in any given day. Use this list of assorted advice to get more accomplished, save your sanity, and feel less rushed. Your family life and your business day will improve.

- Plan for the morning the night before by packing lunches, preparing backpacks and briefcases, and setting aside easy breakfast items such as bagels, waffles, and cereal.

- Shop less often—monthly for staples, weekly for perishables. Keep a running grocery list/errand list on the refrigerator for everyone to contribute to.

- Set aside that cooking day I described previously, and do laundry one or two days each week. Ask family members to pre-soak stains, fold, and put away their own laundry.

- Prioritize and plan. Take some quiet time to focus on things that will move you forward, in household affairs and in business. Make sure that you are meeting deadlines, providing service, bringing in revenue. Determine which aspects of your business do not require your time and talent. Then hire these out.

- Give your children a half-hour to an hour of your uninterrupted time each day. Make it a habit to focus on them and their needs, including their homework, school projects, catch-up conversation, or cuddling together.

- Use call-coding to identify telephone calls, and thus, save time gathering data for client reimbursement. Many long-distance carriers offer this service, and it saves confusion when the bill arrives.

- Cancel unnecessary subscriptions, get yourself off of mailing lists, and throw away junk mail. These all waste time.

- Label wires and connections on computers, phones or other electronic equipment prior to moving it from one location to another. This saves time and frustration when setting it back up again.

- Answer correspondence by hand-writing your response in the margins of the original note.

- Handle paperwork only once. Read it and act on it. Either it gets tossed, filed, or sent back.

- Use a scanner for large volumes of material that you might otherwise have to key in yourself. Sometimes you can scan information at the local copy or printing center if you don't already own a scanner.

- Eliminate follow-up calls or paperwork by making responses a snap for your clients or customers. If you need them to sign off on something, put it in writing, typed out on white paper that could be easily photocopied onto their letterhead. Then, include a self-addressed, stamped envelope or a fax number, as well.

- Highlight frequently called numbers in your telephone directories. And create your own "yellow pages" with a three-ring binder sectioned off with headings like "airlines," "restaurants," "repair services," or whatever listings serve your business and family needs.

- Keep a list of things you can do in five minutes or less. Next time you're on hold on the telephone, or you have a few minutes before leaving for an appointment, check a few things off that list. Your list could include filing, straightening your desk, reading over correspondence, or stuffing envelopes.

- Develop a reading file. Keep it by the door, or in the car, or next to your handbag. Next time you're waiting in a doctor's office, killing time at karate lessons, or sitting in traffic, you'll have articles and clippings you can finish.

- Use online chat rooms to gather colleagues, customers, or clients together—that is, providing you all use the same online service.

- You don't have to let flight time be wasted time. If you travel on business, read, plan for meetings, fill out expense reports, or do some writing. Take advantage of airline clubs that offer business privileges. Becoming a member of these costs money, but it's worth it if you travel frequently. Some airports offer out-of-the-way stations with phones and places to plug in your laptop computer.
- Keep track of credit card numbers, expiration dates, and phone numbers for cancellation if they should be stolen, by photocopying the cards. Do the same to the reverse side, or write in the information. Keep this paper in a secure, separate location for travel.
- Spare future time, effort, and expense by doing a job right the first time.

Mastering money without becoming miserly

If you like a challenge, try to look at building your savings as just that—a game; a challenge to succeed. It does take money to make money sometimes, but if you get into the habit of paying yourself first, that is, writing checks to yourself each month for a savings account, or better yet, establishing an automatic withdrawal, you will be well-served. And when you finally pay off a debt or cash in that unexpected windfall, bank the money. Pretend you are still paying the monthly installment, only pay it into your own bank account. Dollar cost averaging this way really pays off.

Finally, if the temptation to spend unnecessarily is too strong, make your money harder to get at. Lock your money market checkbook in a safe deposit box. Put your credit cards in a bowl of water in the freezer. You will think before spending on impulse purchases. And your money will work for you, not the other way around.

Seasonal sensations

To take advantage of end-of-the-season sales, you may need to change the way you shop. For instance, let's say it's September or October, and as your child starts off to school, you foresee the need for a new winter coat. But what if last year's coat still fits? If your son or daughter can get two months wear out of the coat or jacket, chances are good you'll find better prices in the days following Christmas or during January inventory reductions.

The same approach works when you stock up on swimsuits, beach towels, shorts and sandals in August and September, instead of April and May. Some stores might discount Halloween costumes November 1. Stock up on some, even buying them a bit bigger.

Outfitting kids for less

As any working parent knows, there are periods throughout the year when the budget is taxed with business and personal expenses. Outfitting the kids, especially at back-to-school season, is one of those times.

In her book *Raising Happy Kids On a Reasonable Budget,* Patricia Gallagher says the eleventh commandment should be, "Thou shalt never pay full price for anything." There's no reason to tax your budget when you can opt for end-of-the-season bargains, yard sales, outlets and warehouse stores, consignment shops, and swapping kids' clothing with friends or relatives.

Sudden surprises

"Garage sales are the cheapest places where you can buy clothes— usually about half the price of thrift shops," writes Amy Dacyczyn in *The Tightwad Gazette,* one of the books in her three-volume series. "Instead of thinking about what a shop doesn't have, look at what it does have," she says. "Develop a notebook for your needs, especially if you are shopping for a large family."

Don't let minor flaws or repairs dissuade you from purchasing. Who hasn't worn a brand-new garment, only to have a thread pull loose or a button fall off? If restitching a seam or sewing on a button is all that's necessary, consider the item a true find. In fact, when I was looking for a casual coat to wear with jeans and sweaters, I headed straight for the January clearance rack at my local coat factory outlet. In perfectly flattering colors, I found a coat that was only missing two buttons. One extra button was attached inside as a spare anyway, and I discovered the other in one of the pockets! The coat cost under $10—a real steal!

Retail can be reasonable

If you shop for brand-new merchandise, take advantage of stores that guarantee your purchases. As a mom of two boys, I know the knees wear out first in any jeans or sweat pants I buy. Sears will replace any clothing that wears out before they outgrow them, in the same size you purchased.

Business trip packing list

What with making sure the kids' schedules are taken care of, childcare arrangements are in place, and everything else you have to take care of before a business trip, you often confront last-minute frazzle as you toss your stuff into the suitcase a half-hour before you have to leave. Once you arrive at your destination, you discover you've left behind something essential. Start with this list, and adapt it, to help you save time (and remember the essentials):

- Tickets, passport, airline mileage card.
- Travelers checks, credit cards, cash.
- Zippered pencil pouch or mega-sized paper clip for travel documents.
- Travel office kit (stapler, tape, sticky notes, etc.).
- Luggage cart.
- Reading material and business files.
- Attire for business appointments, with matching accessories.
- Leisure clothes (including comfortable shoes).
- Medications, sunscreen, sunglasses.
- Alarm clock.
- Toiletries, cosmetics, shaving kit.
- Swimsuit, sleep clothes, or jacket/coat if required.
- Small sewing kit, lint brush, plastic bags for laundry.
- Collapsible nylon suitcase to tote home laundry or bulky materials.
- _____
- _____
- _____

Remember that a carry-on bag with wheels is of great value when you are rushing for transportation and don't wish to wait for baggage claim.

Conference costs and concerns

Attending professional conferences is a real opportunity for the home worker in many ways. It gets us out of our offices, and into the broader world of our colleagues. Studies have indicated, however, that if you don't use information you've obtained within three days of a conference, chances are good you won't use that knowledge at all. Because our time and funds are generally tighter than our corporate counterparts, I wanted to add some tips here.

- See if a friend or fellow colleague could also attend the conference and perhaps share the expense of a hotel room and any cab fare to and from the site.
- Offer your services as a volunteer, staffing a registration table or helping in another capacity in return for discounted (perhaps free) admission to the conference. Extra benefit is the additional networking you'll do and goodwill you'll build.
- Keep a to-do list handy as you attend lectures or workshops.
- Dine or socialize with different people at each opportunity to maximize networking possibilities.
- Upon your return, do something immediately with the new material. Expand your Rolodex. Even if you file papers for future use, it's better than letting them go to waste.
- Seek out future opportunities in your field or business, and get to know other important contacts. Your library should have a copy of the *Encyclopedia of Associations*. Use this to find future conferences.

Maximizing technology and minimizing cost

Telephones, fax machines, and computers don't have to take a huge chunk out of your cash flow. Here are some cost-cutting hints:

- Send your faxes after five to be charged the evening rate.
- Invest in a telephone headset if you find that you can accomplish multiple tasks while having your hands free and discussing business matters simultaneously.

- Think twice before installing a toll-free number. Reports from businesses with toll-free lines suggest that less than 40 percent of the callers place orders. The remainder use the number to obtain information, complain, or register comments.
- Leave voice mail messages for people after normal business hours rather than run up your bill with small talk and polite courtesies. You'll get your information across in less time, with less cost.
- Cellular phones are a wonderful use of technology in emergencies or when you absolutely must make an important call while you are out of the office. But if you give your cellular phone number out to everyone, you'll end up paying for their convenience, not yours.
- If using a modem, invest in a higher speed. The added expense will actually pay for itself in less online time or telephone expense.
- Consider using flashsessions for the retrieval of electronic mail. Compose messages off-line, transmit them, and read incoming mail at less expense.
- If you have a lot of technology in your home office—and who doesn't have at least some—consider having a whole-house surge protector, in addition to the powerstrip surge protectors your cords plug into. These can save you hundreds of dollars in appliance or computer replacement or repair costs.

Top 10 ways to save on office supplies

1. Buy briefcases in January or July clearance sales, or when stores reduce their prices around graduation and Father's Day. Outlet stores offer good prices, too.
2. Shop at office superstores (Office Depot, Staples, Office Max) and purchase store brand supplies, including copier paper, legal pads, and tape, for a lower price.
3. Stock up on office supplies during September or October when prices are generally lower because of the back-to-school discounts.

4. Order your checks through check printing services (such as Current catalog) as you'll pay perhaps half of what banks typically charge.

5. Stock up on holiday cards and stationery for next year's greetings immediately after Christmas or during January. Also look for sales on fine engraved stationery during the first of the year when many companies discount for their wedding invitation customers.

6. Purchase individual business greeting cards from large drugstore chains, which typically discount the price of all cards, including business thank-you notes, congratulations cards, and the like.

7. Select telephones from office superstores or electronics stores (such as Circuit City) rather than telephone retail stores. And next time you purchase a telephone, consider a model with a built-in timer to monitor the time spent on long distance calls.

8. When buying a computer, stay one step *behind* the latest technology. You'll find you are still upgrading your present system, but you won't be paying top dollar either. Make your selections from large computer or electronic stores, or consider mail-order catalog companies.

9. Buy books from superstores such as Borders or Barnes & Noble, or use a discount card at chains like B. Dalton or Waldenbooks. If you find yourself purchasing a large quantity of books, join a national book club (Doubleday, Literary Guild, Book of the Month Club, or Writer's Digest Book Club). As a club member, you can specify the type of books (business, reference, etc.) you are most interested in. Check the smaller clubs, run as offshoots of larger clubs: The Money book club features many professional and business books.

10. Use your library for magazines you enjoy reading but don't need to own. If you belong to an online service, check out the free access to the magazines online. If you do want to subscribe, opt for the offers of Publisher's Clearing House or American Family (the sweepstakes companies), or if you are eligible for an educational discount, pick up one of those order forms at your nearby college or university.

Saving on paper and printing

- Use both sides of the paper whenever possible, and use standard sizes as well.

- Make sure all of your copy is correct. Proofread several times, even reading backwards to catch mistakes.

- Paper costs rise periodically, so it's worth it to economize and recycle. For rough drafts or notes, recycled sheets that have been printed on one side are great (see Chapter 3 for more earth-friendly tips).

- Many printers offer discounts if you print a particular color on a certain day of the week, or if you go with one of their standard colors.

- If you are aiming for variety of color, consider changing the percentage of color instead of adding a totally new color to the job. This cuts costs, yet gives the difference you desire.

- If your printing job requires three-hole punched paper, consider printing on pre-drilled paper, especially if the print run is large (say 500 or more sheets).

- Instead of printing full sheets of paper, see if your message might fit on a postcard. Not only will you be saving on printing and paper, but you'll see a reduction in your postage expenses as well.

- When operating your own laser printer in your home office, always have a back-up toner cartridge available. Sell the used cartridge or have it recharged.

- Store toner cartridges in dark, cool places, and store them flat, not standing on end. Properly stored, these can last up to two years if the foil wrapper hasn't been removed.

- Removing your cartridge from the printer occasionally adds life to it. Holding it horizontally, rock it gently from side to side as this redistributes the toner powder more evenly.

More ways to stretch the business dollar

- Always ask new clients or customers how they have heard of you. This often-forgotten question tells whether your marketing dollars have been well spent.

- Be countercyclical. Arrange for improvements to your office space while contractors and painters are waiting out the winter months.

- Consider using co-op advertising to stretch your marketing budget. Co-op advertising splits the cost between you and a franchise parent company, for instance. You can find such opportunities through the salespeople or suppliers you deal with. Co-op advertising can supply you with ready-made ads, flyers, even newsletters that you customize with your name and logo. Just review the requirements, maintain careful records, and make sure that the ads fit into your overall marketing strategy.

- Switch from high-test gasoline to regular unleaded.

- Pay insurance premiums annually instead of monthly where you might often be charged a service fee for the convenience of 12 installments.

- Use small claims court to solve simple legal matters rather than run up large attorney bills. Disputes such as uncollected invoices and work not satisfactorily completed are perfect for this type of adjudication. You must file within the district where the incident occurred or where the person you're suing resides or conducts business. Usually the dollar amount cannot exceed a limit (sometimes $8,000), or the matter is referred to Common Pleas Court.

- Shop around for a credit card that does not charge an annual fee, or one with a better interest rate (remember, interest on business purchases is tax deductible, though not on personal expenditures). Or ask your credit card company to lower your rate. If they see you're ready to move your business, they just might accommodate you.

- Get full value for your postage expenses. Rarely do first-class billings contain more than one sheet of paper. Use this as a chance to communicate with customers and clients by sending along a newsletter, a personal note, or information they might appreciate.

- Add the line "or current resident" to your direct mailing labels. This way, if your intended recipient has moved away, your mail won't end up in the dead letter office, and someone has a chance of reading it.

- Use the library or a lending service of a professional organization you might belong to rather than purchase expensive materials you need to review. Computer user's groups can alert you to shareware and freeware rather than expensive software.

- If you must purchase software (if you have an outdated version of the application), upgrades generally cost less.

- Meet a client for breakfast or lunch instead of dinner. These meals are less expensive, and if you meet for breakfast, you might both be more efficient with your time.

- Use next-afternoon or second-day service for lower rates on packages unless it absolutely must be there by the next morning.

- Ask for business discounts, if they are available. Complain if you are not satisfied with the service.

- Barter services with other professionals or businesses, especially when it works out to be a win-win situation for each party involved.

- Hire your spouse or children as employees. There are tax advantages. (See Chapter 9.)

- Write to the Consumer Information Center for free information available to business owners. Booklets such as "Starting a Business" and "Running a Small Business" are free. Others are available at minimal cost. Ask for a catalog (P.O. Box 100, Pueblo, CO 81002) or pick one up at your library.

Finding affordable health insurance

If you're married, your best option is to maintain health coverage on your spouse's plan (assuming your spouse is not self-employed, too). Barring that, try joining large professional organizations that offer group rates to self-employed professionals or small businesses. Many chambers of commerce offer this as a benefit to their members. You might also check with your local small business economic development office for referrals.

If you are leaving a full-time position with benefits, you could choose the COBRA option since employers must carry you on the policy for 18 months after your departure (at your cost, of course). In cases where your spouse may have had benefits and you are divorcing, the COBRA period is even longer than 18 months.

However, if none of these options works for you, you'll have to shop for a health-care insurance policy as you cannot afford to be without coverage. An accident or illness could very well wipe you out financially. There are providers that offer individual plans to people during open enrollment periods. Many of these plans are with preferred provider organizations (PPOs), which require you to select from a list of health-care providers.

What to look for in any plan you choose? Make sure you're given a choice of deductibles, sufficient coverage for outpatient services, prescription, dental or vision coverage (if you need it), and coverage for major operations or transplants. Before signing with any insurance carrier you are not familiar with, be sure it is financially sound. A quick check with your state's insurance department can put your mind at ease. Sometimes it is difficult to find good quality health care plans at an affordable cost if you are self-employed, and not a part of a larger group policy. Check to see if you'll be paying extremely high deductibles to cover somewhat common conditions such as asthma.

Building your savings

There's no great secret to money management, but it's a good idea to follow a few simple rules:

1. Think before you spend.
2. Limit access to your disposable income.
3. Live beneath your means.
4. Pay yourself first.
5. Keep track of your expenses.
6. Learn all you can about personal finance.
7. Diversify your investments.
8. Invest for the long-term.

Resources

Raising Happy Kids On a Reasonable Budget by Patricia C. Gallagher (Betterway).

The Tightwad Gazette (Volumes I, II, and III) by Amy Dacyczyn (Villiard).

Beardstown Ladies' Guide to Smart Spending for Big Savings—How to Save for a Rainy Day Without Sacrificing Your Lifestyle (Hyperion).

The Frugal Entrepreneur by Terri Lonier (Portico Press).

Money-Smart Secrets for the Self-Employed by Linda Stern (Random House).

Government Giveaways for Entrepreneurs I, II, and *III* by Matthew Lesko (Information USA).

The Second Shift by Arlie Hochschild (Viking).

The Time Bind: When Work Becomes Home and Home Becomes Work by Arlie Hochschild (Metropolitan Books).

Hints from Heloise (Avon Books).

Is There Life After Housework? by Don Aslett (F&W Publications).

Household Hints & Handy Tips (Reader's Digest).

How to Make the Most of Your Workday by Jonathan and Susan Clark (Career Press).

You Can Find More Time for Yourself Every Day by Stephanie Culp (F&W Publications).

Never Call Your Broker On Monday by Nancy Dunnan (Harper Perennial).

101 Ways to Grow Your Business with Barter by Kirk Whisler and Jim Sullivan (WPR Publishing).

1001 Ways to Cut Your Expenses by Jonathan D. Pond (Dell).

Money Smarts, the Guide to Saving Money—325 Valuable Tips That Will Help You Stretch Your Dollars by David L. Scott (Globe Pequot).

The Smart Woman's Guide to Spending, Saving and Managing Money by Diane Pearl and Ellie Williams Clinton (Career Press).

The Financially Confident Woman by Mary Hunt (Broadman & Holman).

Women & Money by Frances Leonard (Addison Wesley).

Time Is Money by Frances Leonard (Addison Wesley).

Time Management for Dummies by Jeffrey J. Mayer (IDG Books).

Marshall Loeb's Lifetime Financial Strategies (Little Brown).

The Essential Business Buyer's Guide by the staff of *Business Consumer Guide* (Sourcebooks).

Mom, Can I Have That? Dr. Tightwad Answers Your Kids' Questions About Money by Janet Bodnar (Kiplinger).

Never Pay Retail edited by Sid Kirshheimer (Rodale).

Money Magazine and *Kiplinger's Personal Finance Magazine.*

Chapter 7

Choosing childcare that's right for you

Home-based entrepreneurs are faced with special challenges and circumstances when arranging childcare. For instance, it's not as easy to have in-home care while you try to work on the premises. Even though someone else may be there to care for the children, kids naturally gravitate toward their parents.

Parents are often shocked to discover that while the United States sets standards for highways, seat belts, drugs, and food, there are no national standards for childcare. Although individual states regulate the quality of childcare centers, knowing what's available, what questions to ask, and what concerns to consider helps to speed the process and ensure happy, healthy childcare arrangements.

There really are many types of childcare available to you and your children. There's a private sitter, often a grandparent or other relative who can watch your child in your house or in theirs. A popular alternative is organized childcare in a licensed center. Another solution is the family day-care home where a childcare worker cares for several children in a private residence.

But even when a suitable arrangement presents itself, various work-related obstacles and personal challenges get in the way. Children might become ill. Your job may require you to be out of town. Perhaps your child is physically or mentally challenged, requiring specialized care. You may be surprised to learn that these childcare challenges can be overcome as well. This chapter is designed to help you sort through options you may not have been aware of.

Of course, no one can care for your children as well as you do, but your at-home job may demand that you have full-time—or part-time if your kids are in school—childcare. Whatever your needs, it's important to come to terms with your situation and make the arrangements that work best for you.

Hiring in-home caregivers

If your mother, another close relative, or a friend is your in-home caregiver, you probably have a pretty high comfort level with the quality of care your child will be getting, and feel little need to interview this individual or set out the ground rules.

However, it's not a bad idea, in this circumstance, to establish some basic expectations, both in terms of your availability during your workday and in terms of rules for the kids. That way, you'll avoid future conflicts ("Oh, I didn't think you'd mind if Jenny had a box of chocolate candy right before nap time.")

Explain why you feel particular incidents should be handled in a certain way. In cases where children have food allergies, attention span deficits, or behavioral problems, your mom might not be aware of the challenges and what the child's doctors, counselors, or teachers advocate.

If you're considering a stranger as an in-home caregiver, you'll definitely want to interview and get references. If you haven't had much hiring experience, your discomfort is natural. You might want to begin the screening process by developing your own job application in which you can ask questions that you need answers to, but might feel uneasy asking. Such questions could include:

- Do you have your own transportation?

- Are you an organized person? Patient? A good housekeeper?

- Do you have any health-related conditions (physical limitations, allergies, etc.) that would affect your work?
- What was your last childcare experience? Why did it end? Are there any other experiences with young children you can talk about?
- Have you ever had to handle a crisis or emergency? How did you deal with it?
- What do you like best about working with children? Least?
- Do you have a driver's license? Have you received any tickets or citations, and if so, for what? Has your license ever been revoked?
- Have you ever been convicted of any crimes?
- Have you ever received first aid or CPR training?

In addition, you probably want to find out a little about the personality, likes, and dislikes of any person working in your home. Ask:

- Do you smoke? Drink?
- What do you like to do for relaxation?
- What are your favorite books? Television shows? Music?
- What are your strengths or the things you like about yourself? What about weaknesses or areas for improvement?
- How would you handle a crying baby? A toddler's tantrum?
- Would you be willing to provide transportation to and from music lessons or dance class? Could you occasionally supervise when my child has a friend over?
- What do you think makes for a happy childhood?

Your list of questions might differ, but the point is to use the written application to screen potential caregivers, and make subsequent discussion easier. Always ask for at least three references, and state clearances for those who work with children (in Pennsylvania that's called Act 33/34 Clearance).

If you're particularly anxious about screening candidates in person, ask in your ad that potential caregivers send a self-addressed, stamped envelope with their letter. This way you can begin reviewing their resumes while they complete the application you mail back to them.

The *au pair* alternative

Another option for at-home childcare is to hire an *au pair*, typically a young woman from Europe or elsewhere outside the United States. An *au pair* is brought to the United States as part of an intercultural exchange. While some *au pairs* may do light household tasks related to the children's care (preparing meals, cleaning up, laundering children's clothes, and taking them to lessons or appointments), an *au pair* is not a housekeeper.

Parents admit that the hidden benefit to their *au pair* program is the cultural exchange—the chance to expose their children to another culture and language (although most *au pairs* speak fluent English). The family also benefits from watching their caretaker react to American culture. Besides in-home convenience and the cultural perspectives, what are some advantages and disadvantages of having an *au pair*?

"You have to have an open mind that what you're getting is another family member," says Michael, a Pennsylvania father of two daughters who employed an *au pair*. "This is not a person who disappears at five o'clock, and you have to be prepared for that. She has her own space, but we do a lot of things together. We watch TV and prepare meals together. It's really a team effort." Michael points out that families do lose a little privacy and that it's essential to communicate your expectations, remembering that primary responsibility is for the children, not you.

Most *au pair* programs have a limit to the number of hours these caregivers work, usually around 40 to 45 hours per week. For families requiring more time, the *au pair* alternative might pose problems. But many say it's comparable to what they were paying for their children in organized, off-site childcare.

Jean Quinn is director of development for the InterExchange Au Pair USA program. She says families pay an upfront application fee of $4,080, which covers the screening and transatlantic airfare for the *au pair*. In addition, a $128-a-week stipend is paid to the au pair and, usually, another $500 in tuition is required so that the *au pair* can partake of educational opportunities in the US.

A separate bedroom for an *au pair* must be provided, per government regulations, but bathrooms can be shared.

Selecting group care

Day-care centers. Start your selection by preparing a list of questions to ask during your initial telephone screening. How many children attend? How old are they? What is the ratio of staff to children? Most experts agree that there should be no more than four infants to one adult, five toddlers to one adult and 10 preschoolers to one adult.

What level of education do the center's providers have? What are the rates? Do they change as your child gets older and requires less one-on-one care? Are lunches or snacks provided? What activities are there? What discipline methods are used? How secure is the building and playground? What's the turnover rate for the center's staff?

State and local governments license childcare centers. The National Association for the Education of Young Children (NAEYC) has an accreditation program for centers that exceeds the requirements of state regulatory systems. Such accreditation is not mandatory but it is a sign that the center is working to provide the very best of service. To find an accredited center in your area, you can call NAEYC at 800-424-2460.

Family-care setting. The same considerations for childcare centers apply to family day-care providers and sites, but the questions do become a bit more personal. For instance, don't hesitate to say, "Tell me about yourself," or ask, "Would you please describe your childcare experience for me?" Ask about registration with the state or local government. Is any extra help provided, and if so, who provides it? How many children are cared for altogether? How many days was the provider ill within the past year? Does he or she smoke? Are there any pets around? Are there any disabilities that would interfere with the care of your child? How does the family of the provider feel about the job and the children? Why did the provider begin the business in the first place?

Other things you might want to consider are physical surroundings, where the children eat, nap, play, and learn. Look for health precautions (frequent hand washing especially), childproofing, emergency procedures that are posted, books, and educational equipment. Find out what activities go on and if the provider takes the children places (such as the library or to the park). Ask the caregiver how he or she would react in certain situations (if your child is choking, if there is a discipline problem, etc.).

Mister Rogers on choosing childcare

"If I were looking for day care for my child," writes TV's Fred Rogers in *Mister Rogers Talks with Parents*, "there are several things I'd want to be sure of—as sure as I possibly could be.

"First of all, I'd want to know if the people offering day care had experience with both the emotional and physical needs of very young children. Where else have they worked? What makes them qualified to look after infants and toddlers?

"I'd want to be assured that one specific person in that day-care center was going to be responsible for my particular baby every day. It would be important to me to know that my baby would be adjusting to only one main caretaker besides myself.

"If I were dropping off a toddler, I'd look around to make sure there were plenty of toddler-type spaces, toys and activities as well as the things that infants need. I'd want someone to be in charge of my toddler who didn't have to be in charge of infants as well.

"I'd want to feel that the person taking care of my child really cared about *my* relationship with my child, was a kind of parenting partner with me, and understood that these times of separation were difficult for both my child *and* me. If I couldn't feel these things, I'd look for somewhere and someone else.

"If you've already been out looking for day care for your child, you'll probably have learned that my few 'wants' are really hard to find in one place. If you can find them, it may be an expensive day-care service. It is not only sad but *serious* that there are so few healthy alternatives for working mothers."

Fred Rogers and his staff at Family Communications feel so strongly about the importance of quality childcare in homes and in centers that they've developed the Mister Rogers' Child Care Partnership, available through PBS stations around the country. Originally started as a pilot project with grant money from the Corporation for Public Broadcasting, the childcare initiative has proved tremendously successful.

The project emphasizes viewing *Mister Rogers' Neighborhood* with the children and includes talking and playing about it afterward, with suggestions from the *Mister Rogers' Plan & Play Book,* a training videotape, and a free quarterly newsletter.

"We found that the children became less hostile, kinder and more imaginative in their play, and that child-care providers grew professionally, becoming more patient, more attentive to emotional and social concerns, that they had more reasonable expectations and felt valued in their work," says Hedda Sharapan, associate producer with Family Communications. "It was heartwarming to think that we could be a source of support to them."

Portions of *Mister Rogers Talks with Parents* by Fred Rogers and Barry Head, reprinted with permission. © 1983, Family Communications, Inc.

Special-needs children

My youngest son, Alex, was born severely premature with chronic lung disease. This put him at risk for serious complications caused by a simple cold virus. At this writing, he's still not totally outgrown the condition. So I wanted to keep him out of organized childcare and the germs of other children for as many years possible.

I had to realize that I couldn't do everything. I limited my work to projects I could complete on a flexible schedule from the confines of my home. In fact, I found it necessary to give up a client when I simply couldn't attend the necessary meetings. Nap times were sacred. That's when I really sat down to work. The same with favorite half-hour television programs that captured his attention.

If you need to provide specialized care (as I did with breathing treatments or when the physical therapist came to the house), you could employ an in-home caregiver for the periods when you aren't directly needed for the child's care. Your sitter could supervise, play with, and feed your child while you are in your home office. You'll be within easy access if any special needs arise.

If your child is a bit older and his or her needs are not as critical, you may seek the help of outside day care. Carefully research and investigate centers you are considering. Some centers aren't equipped to handle children with physical disabilities, and some caregivers aren't experienced enough to help your child with other disorders.

Probably the most difficult children to find spaces for are those with significant behavioral problems. Ask about the staff's training and the group size. You may need to talk with several directors before you'll find one who will accept your child. That in itself can make any parent very anxious. You might also ask administrators of the school district and local chamber of commerce and your pediatrician for leads on specialized childcare.

Childcare when your child is ill

Most in-home caregivers will still come to your home if your child's illness is minor, so it's usually lost days at group day care you have to plan for.

The scenario is fairly common: You have an important meeting tomorrow morning. Your child comes to you with those dreaded words, "I feel sick." You run for the thermometer and check your child's status every hour. If the condition persists or worsens, you know you will have to sacrifice your day's plans unless you've made previous arrangements.

Where I live, parents who face this predicament register their children with the Get Well Room, a department of the Children's Center of Pittsburgh. It provides a warm, loving place for children to recuperate from mild illnesses such as sore throats, colds, mild bronchitis, diarrhea, or pain and fever from vaccinations. Staffed by a registered nurse, the room is available for children whose parents have preregistered. If the center is not filled on the morning you call, your child can spend the day.

Parents report that at the Get Well Room, children get more one-on-one care than they'd get in a normal day-care setting. There are aides to help the pediatric nurse, and activities are very low key, involving reading, watching videotapes or sleeping, if need be. With the number of parents working, plenty wish there were more alternatives like this.

If you don't have a similar setting near you to rely upon when your child is ill, devise a contingency plan that might include family, friends, neighbors, or some people from your house of worship to assist you.

Easing separation anxiety

It's not uncommon for youngsters to have a certain amount of separation anxiety when starting day care, and it usually fades as your child gets used to the routine. Such anxiety, especially for toddlers, shows that your child is a little torn between his need for independence and his dependence on you.

How to find baby sitters

Parents need to consider the age and energy level of a sitter, the qualifications that go into the baby-sitting responsibility, and any references that can be provided. Simply put, are rambunctious toddlers going to wear out older people or put teenagers to tests they aren't ready for? Whomever you choose should be able to handle a variety of situations that might arise, including feeding, bathing, and disciplining your children, as well as any emergency measures such as choking rescue procedures, mouth-to-mouth breathing, and cardiopulmonary resuscitation (CPR).

This business of selecting a sitter is serious, but it doesn't have to be difficult. If you're comfortable with friends and relatives, you may have already found a first-rate sitter, providing these people want to baby-sit.

As children get older, you can use teenage sitters during mealtimes and throughout the evenings, whereas with very young children, you might feel more comfortable with adults. For overnights, you may prefer relatives.

Perhaps you can find the help you need from neighbors, teenage baby sitters or programs near you. Also try asking friends, day-care workers or those in your house of worship's office for their recommendations. It's usually best to use someone you know, or at least know of, through someone else. Otherwise call upon youth groups, Girl Scout troops, or the YWCA/YWHA to see if they have a list of qualified sitters.

Certainly there are some situations that require more thought to baby-sitting arrangements than others. Infants require gentle care and knowledge that only more mature sitters can offer. Children with medical concerns might be better left in the hands of relatives or caregivers with special training. When I found a nursing student willing to baby-sit, I felt much better leaving Alex for brief stints, and even scheduled a weekend getaway.

To ease the stress of separation anxiety, schedule a pre-enrollment site visit to familiarize your youngster with caregivers. Remember that children need support, and not necessarily sympathy. The minute they see they are succeeding at making you feel sorry for them, they won't have much incentive to change their bid for your attention.

Give your little one a hug, tell him about the fun things on the agenda that day, give him or her something to look forward to when you return, and depart. Make a swift exit, and perhaps check back with the teacher by phone later in the day. Folks who pop their heads in later on "just to check" make matters worse by doing so.

If your youngster is attached to a favorite doll, stuffed animal, or blanket, let him or her tote that item along for security. Or encourage your child to bring an object for "show and tell." Never scold your child for feeling the way he or she does, but don't let it eat away at you. In time your child will most likely assimilate with the other children.

Baby-sitter training

There are baby-sitting courses offered throughout the country and in communities near you. You might want to suggest this to the teen up the street who lacks experience yet displays wonderful enthusiasm toward your children.

Safe Sitter, a program begun in 1980 by Indianapolis pediatrician, Dr. Patricia A. Keener, strives to increase the availability of safe, nurturing adolescent caregivers. With more than 550 participating hospitals and teaching sites in 48 states, the program is easily accessed by calling 800-255-4089. Any boy or girl age 11 to 13, can sign up for a baby-sitting course near them.

Presbyterian University Hospital in Pittsburgh is a participant in the Safe Sitter Program. "Taking a course like this does make a sitter a better parent in the future," says Lea Ann Ostergaard, health promotion coordinator. The course is offered in two eight-hour sessions and covers the business of baby-sitting, choking and rescue breathing, accident management, and safety tips. Those wanting CPR certification are referred to an additional class. For only $10, teens are armed with materials and knowledge. There is a written and a hands-on test for certain skills and much practice—everything from telephone calls that arrange sitting to diapering a baby.

Top 10 list to leave any caregiver

So you've found a sitter you feel comfortable with? Before you walk out the door, be sure to give your baby sitter a brief walk-through of your home, pointing out these things (not necessarily ranked in order of importance):

1. Location of telephone, with emergency numbers for police, fire, ambulance, pediatrician, and poison control center nearby. In fact, it's very convenient for sitters if you have all of this information on a luggage tag attached to your child's diaper bag.

2. The telephone directory, along with the names and numbers of neighbors or relatives who could back you up in an emergency.

3. Instructions for reaching you. This is when a personal pager or cellular phone is most valuable.

4. The location of your fire extinguisher and first aid kit.

5. Allowable snacks and drinks and forbidden treats (those that pose a choking or allergy hazard). "I usually prepare whatever they're to have to eat so it's all ready to serve, sitting in the refrigerator," says one mom I know who has three children with food allergies.

6. Any medicine the children require, with instructions of when to give it, how much, and how to measure the dosage. Sitters should also know where to take the child for medical treatment, the name of your pediatrician, and the insurance information (unless you know this is on file at the hospital or doctor's office).

7. Restrictions as to the use of the phone, television, video games, music, and friends invited over. This same list could apply not only for the children, but for the hired sitter as well.

8. Tasks that must be completed by your kids. Your list might include homework, books to be read before bed, or toys to be picked up.

9. A copy of *Kid Sitter Basics: A Handbook for Babysitters* by Celeste Stuhring, R.N. Included are suggestions for games, tips on getting the little ones to bed, emergency procedures, potential hazards, and handy checklists for parents to leave behind for their baby sitters.

10. A script (written or not) of what to say if others call. For instance, you may want teenage sitters to say, "Mrs. Smith can't come to the phone right now, but I can take your name and number and she'll get back to you when she can."

"I personally would want my sitters to have this training," says Ostergaard, herself the mother of two active boys. The course requires the commitment of time and money, but young people often report that having the training puts parents more at ease and increases their baby-sitting income.

Picking a preschool

The keys to a successful preschool experience include the fit between the child's personality and the nature of the preschool, the convenience of the location, the schedule, and the cost. A good preschool can greatly enhance your child's development, building a foundation and love of learning for years to come. Conversely, a poor arrangement wreaks havoc on family routines and creates more stress than anything else.

Start your selection by deciding upon the type of preschool philosophy you might like for your child:

- Cooperative programs require varying degrees of parental involvement, and might not be conducive to the work-at-home parent who needs childcare as part of the preschool function.

- Developmental preschools assist children with specific needs, and tend to be more nonacademic. For instance, my youngest son qualified for the DART developmental preschool when he was 3. There he received weekly physical therapy and speech therapy that helped him catch up with his typically developing peers.

- Montessori or Waldorf classrooms are two specific types of preschools you may also choose. Mixed-age classrooms, extended periods of free play, and teaching materials that require minimal teacher direction are hallmarks of the Montessori approach. Children here are encouraged to develop at their own pace.

   With Waldorf, parents find a strong emphasis on the arts and nature, using mixed-age classrooms and simple materials or toys. Here children are thought to learn through imitating adult behavior.

- Academic settings stress early reading, beginning computation, and other skills reserved for early elementary school.

- Religious preschools vary in the degree of religious instruction they offer. Some are merely sponsored by a local church, but welcome children of other denominations; some are reserved for the followers of a certain faith.

Friends, family, and neighbors can all become referral sources when you seek a preschool for your child. Once you've identified one or more preschools you want to consider, set aside enough time for a visit. Here are some things to look out for:

- The National Association for the Education of Young Children (NAEYC) recommends that at least one staff member at any preschool hold a degree in early-childhood education.

- Look at the ratio of students to teachers. For a class of 3-year-olds, there should be one teacher for every six children. That ratio widens as children get older.

- Observe the interaction between the teachers and the youngsters. Do they really listen to the kids? Are children reminded to wash hands after using the rest rooms? Is discipline used as a tool for youngsters to learn self-regulation and better communication, or is it merely a form of punishment?

- Preschool facilities should be bright and cheerful. What adorns the walls? Be cautious of a school where all the artwork looks exactly the same. This could be a sign that the teacher is more interested in running a tight ship than in allowing little ones to express themselves.

- You want a preschool with an open-door policy allowing you to visit whenever you like, but a closed-door policy protecting your little ones. Only one exit should be used to insure children leave with the proper caregiver.

- Toys and equipment should be in good shape, with no tiny parts for the under-3 set.

- Smoke alarms and fire extinguishers should be in clear view.
- Bathrooms should be reduced to a child's scale.

Costs vary, but the NAEYC suggests that you might expect to pay between $4,500 and $10,000 annually for full-time preschool with extended day care (Monday through Friday from 8 a.m. until 6 p.m.). In some areas, you may pay less.

Don't forget to register your child well in advance. Many preschools begin accepting applications for the September school year in February or March.

Single parent relief

A single parent's day sometimes never seems to end. Sometimes I just shake my head and wonder how I do it all.

In her book *Second Chances: Men, Women & Children a Decade After Divorce,* Judith Wallerstein, Ph.D., with her co-author Sandra Blakeslee, says, "Single parenting involves different responsibilities and skills than does parenting as part of an intact couple. There is no one to lean on when times are rough. The parent who raises children alone must be able to live with a great deal of day-to-day anxiety. He or she must take a stand and hold to it, without backup, often in the face of vociferous opposition. He or she must be responsible for children when they're sick, injured, or emotionally upset."

Out-of-town childcare

Increasingly, hotel chains across the country are improving their access to quality childcare, out of courtesy for working parents. Embassy Suites is one chain that has childcare facilities for some business travelers. In 1989, Hyatt Hotels inaugurated "Camp Hyatt," which entertains children ages 3 to 12 at various hotel locations.

If your child is hesitant to attend one of these organized groups, ask the hotel concierge (in advance, of course) about in-room baby-sitting services. Or if need be, plan to travel with a relative or friend who could offer that support for you while you attend to business details. At the end of the day, you can spend time together, and view the experience as a mini-vacation.

As a single mom, I've tried to take advantage of any opportunities for relief, without taking advantage of the people offering such help. From time to time, I've enlisted my parents, my neighbor across the street, or others to help out with the boys.

Check with local religious centers, community centers, and the United Way. There may very well be day-care, or play group programs you can use, at minimal or no cost.

Are childcare expenses tax deductible?

The good news is, your childcare expenses can help lower the bottom line on any tax you owe. Take the Child and Dependent Care Tax Credit on your federal return. Keep careful records of what you pay for childcare. Write checks rather than using cash, and get receipts. On the federal form, you'll also need to provide the IRS with the taxpayer identification number of your day-care center or caregiver.

Another bit of relief, depending upon your income bracket, is the Earned Income Credit, which you might qualify for, especially if you're just getting your business off the ground, and your income falls within the limits.

Resources

Mister Rogers Talks with Parents by Fred Rogers and Barry Head (Family Communications Inc.).

Raising Happy Kids On a Reasonable Budget by Patricia C. Gallagher (Betterway).

On My Own: Helping Kids Help Themselves by Tova Navarra (Barron's).

Kid Sitter Basics: A Handbook for Babysitters by Celeste Stuhring, R.N. (Westport Publishers).

The Babysitter's Handbook by Barbara Benton (Morrow).

Super Sitters: A Complete Home System for You and Your Babysitter by Lee Salk (kit).

A Child's Place: A Year In the Life In a Day Care Center by Ellen Ruppel Shell (Little Brown).

How to Be a Super Sitter by Jay Litvin and Lee Salk (VGM Career Horizons).

Prime Time Together with Kids: Creative Ideas, Activities, Games & Projects by Donna Erickson (Augsburg).

Working Mothers: Strategies for Coping by Jeanne Bodin and Bonni Mitelman (Ballantine).

Playgroups: From 18 Months to Kindergarten—A Complete Guide for Parents by Sheila Wolper and Beth Levine (Pocket Books).

How to Choose a Nursery School: A Parents' Guide to Preschool Education by Ada Anbar (Pacific Books).

Everything You Always Wanted to Know About Preschool but Didn't Know Whom to Ask by Ellen Church (Scholastic).

101 Great Ways to Keep Your Child Entertained While You Get Something Else Done by Danelle Hickman and Valerie Teurlay (St. Martin's Press).

Chapter 8

They're only young once!

Do you remember the stir First Lady Barbara Bush caused when she gave the commencement address at Wellesley College? "At the end of your life, you will never regret not having passed one more test, not winning one more verdict, or not closing one more deal. You will regret time not spent with a husband, a child, a friend, or a parent."

I believe Mrs. Bush was right, and I think more women in my generation are learning that while you can try to combine a career with raising a family, it's awfully tough. If you're pulled in too many directions without the right planning and support, something usually suffers—your marriage, your children, your health and sanity, and certainly your career.

This chapter reinforces the notion that, while parents may grow old with regrets, few will wish they could have spent more time at work. Most will regret lost time with their children and families. As another famous First Lady, the late Jacqueline Kennedy Onassis, commented many years prior, "If you bungle raising your children, I don't think whatever else you do matters very much."

Still, we're professional parents, creatures of the workforce as well as of parenthood. Granted, having a home-based business makes each of these roles just a little bit easier, but you never escape the inherent struggles.

In this chapter, I hope to help alleviate any guilt pangs, enabling you to let go of that which you cannot control, and take charge of circumstances which you can. Learn what your guilt triggers are—lack of time with your children, a messy house, the influences of other people's lifestyle, or criticism from family.

In this chapter are numerous suggestions for activities, games, pastimes, even recipes to help keep your children entertained and, perhaps more important, create opportunities for you to spend special time with them.

Strengthening family ties

A good acquaintance of mine, Hedda, works in the office of Family Communications, the nonprofit company that produces *Mister Rogers' Neighborhood*. As I was writing this book, Hedda shared with me her thoughts about working from home.

"Being able to work from home when my two daughters were young was Fred's gift to me," Hedda says. "It let me be with my children as I needed to be, yet it allowed the professional side of me to grow. I gave up benefits but gained being there when my girls needed me, if they hadn't slept the night before or if they had to come home sick from school." Hedda reports that in those days she took her work everywhere—to the swimming pool, to appointments, and even on some vacations.

But she also remembers a time when her daughter Laurie asked, "Is there ever going to be a time when you don't have work to do?" At that moment, she put down her work and replied, "Would you like that time to be now?" Laurie affirmed her need with a resounding yes.

Admittedly, there may be times when we are completing papers that must be overnighted in an hour, or we have to speak to the caller we've been playing telephone tag with, but in many instances, if we ask ourselves, "What difference will a 15-minute break cause?" we'll find the sacrifice small, but the gesture grand in the minds of our children.

So whenever you feel your child clamoring for your attention, take a brief break, or at least schedule a respite in the very near future. My son Andy and I take a break some evenings to play a game of chess, and Alex loves to bring his toys next to me as I work. Every few minutes we stop to reconnect with a smile or warm word.

Some families make a conscious effort to set aside a family night or day out. Your family night might be going out for pizza or staying at home, spreading a blanket and pillows, making popcorn and watching rented movies.

In other families, all the members pitch in during the week to clean the house, run errands, or help with the laundry so that on Friday or Saturday there is time to take in a movie or simply stroll through the neighborhood. Letting your children decide on the activities also involves them. Board games, good books, and interactive toys help to make this time possible, but you can certainly have fun baking cookies, packing lunches, or enjoying any ordinary activity.

Explaining why you work

Some children simply can't get enough of their parents' time. If you've heard the refrain, "But *why* do you have to work?" then you know what I'm talking about.

I consulted an expert on money matters for this one. Janet Bodnar is better known in her role as "Ask Dr. Tightwad," for she writes the syndicated column. Bodnar is also the author of *Dr. Tightwad's Money-Smart Kids* as well as *Mom, Can I Have That?*

"Tell your children that you work to earn money to pay for all the things your whole family needs and wants," Bodnar writes in her second book. "Tell them you work to earn money to save for the future, to pay for next year's vacation or a new car. Tell them you work because you're good at what you do. Tell them you work because you enjoy it." She emphasizes that, because we parents spend a large chunk of time on the job, anything we can do to help make our kids feel a part of that worklife is welcomed.

One mom, Bodnar points out, took her children on a tour of her home office, explaining what she did there and how her job helped her make money. "Several weeks later [this mom] mentioned that she was short on cash and would have to make a trip to the bank, when her son piped up, 'Mommy, you can just go into your office and make some.'"

Homework for the workaholic

Do you find that the higher you climb the ladder of success, the more hours you seem to be putting in? Do you find your relationships with your children are dwindling to formalities?

It's easy in this era of corporate downsizing and merger mania for all workers to be a little preoccupied with their professional lives. Even the self-employed may be picking up the slack for their corporate clients—the very reason that their counterparts may be farming that work out in the first place.

But realize that too much time spent on the job robs you not only of restful relaxation, but can also impair your judgment and affect your health. The price of workaholism is often measured in terms of a weaker immune system, thereby lowering resistance to infectious disease. Aches and pains mount also.

What's the solution? Simple: Quit work. Not on a permanent basis, of course. But for a moment. An afternoon. A weekend. Here are a few tips for changing your work-haunted habits.

- Engage in physical activity that totally takes your mind off work. For me, it's gardening or lawncare that also allows me to see the direct results of my labor (another psychological boost).

- Use some means to measure your free time. Set a timer. Use the beginning or end of a television newscast or program. But make certain that you use all of the time allotted to relax or do something other than work.

- Learn to feel comfortable turning down work when you know you can't handle it under a reasonable schedule, or at least negotiate a longer deadline.

- Accept the fact that you don't have to complete everything that crosses your desk each day. Sometimes the proverbial night's rest gives you a clearer perspective.

- Commit to spending time away from work. Plan a vacation, schedule a Saturday on the tennis courts or just give yourself the luxury of an afternoon with a good book. Your business will be better for it!

- Limit your workday. Clock out at 5 p.m. and leave your evenings free.
- Before you leave your desk or home office each day, set up guidelines for what you'll tackle tomorrow. That list-making helps you feel a sense of accomplishment in itself.

When baby sets your schedule

Combining a home business with the demands of a newborn or infant is most definitely a challenge, but don't forget your priorities. Number one has to be taking care of the baby, which means frequent nursing and feeding, bathing, changing, and soothing. Number two in the priority list is taking care of you. This one is easy to push aside.

You've heard the old saying, "Sleep when the baby sleeps"? Well in the first few weeks or months you have to. If you aren't well-rested, you have nothing else to give your infant, the rest of the family, and certainly your business efforts. Allow yourself a reasonable maternity leave, even though you might easily put in a few hours of work each day or week.

Enlist help whenever possible in completing the mundane tasks of cooking, cleaning, and running errands. Perhaps family members can pitch in. Friends sometimes provide meals to new moms on an as-needed basis. And you can always hire a cleaning person to help out if the budget allows.

Once the baby—and *you*—begin sleeping through the night, dedicate nap times to getting an hour or two of work accomplished. If you feel household tasks looming, try this: Right before nap time, place baby in a safety seat or baby swing while you tidy up the kitchen or throw in a load of laundry, or even take a quick shower. Just put the baby seat safely on the bathroom floor and keep the shower brief. You can chat with baby, freshen up, and be ready to tackle more work when the baby does fall off to sleep.

Surviving the summer while keeping your cool

Summer is always a struggle. Each year I can feel the panic coming. It's not that I dislike bright sunshine and outdoor activities. I welcome them. But summer presents a whole host of challenges, not the least of which are the added hours my sons are at home and in need of attention from me. I know I need to resort to creative solutions and often need to develop a patchwork plan of childcare, outside care, and a more unstructured work schedule to make it all work. Here are some of the strategies I've resorted to that could work for you, too:

- Be flexible. You won't have as structured a day as when your children are in school. The kids will want to venture outside and they'll likely need closer supervision.

- If you have the advantage of a fenced-in yard, this prevents little ones from wandering off. You'll still want to work nearby, or at least within earshot. (A baby monitor is useful even when your kids are older, for this very reason.)

- If your toddlers are happy playing in the backyard sandbox or wading pool, you can take advantage of the sunshine, too. Pull up a chair and make this your reading time.

- Often sunshine is stymied by summer rain. Depending upon the ages of your children and the limits you set for television, you may find that your youngsters are more than happy to spend some quiet time watching a favorite show or videotape.

- When school's out for *your* kids, that means school's out for teenagers, as well. There might be a responsible neighborhood teen who'd like to earn a little money watching your youngsters for a few hours each day or a couple days each week.

- Consider a day camp program. They're offered for all ages—and there's usually a lot of flexibility in session length. Most programs offer summer-long sessions, as well as shorter increments—a month, six weeks. You may also choose from a variety of specialty camps—from drama and art workshops to sports and nature programs. Camps may be offered by community centers, churches and synagogues, day-care centers, or private organizations.

- If you belong to a health, country, tennis, or golf club with onsite childcare privileges, take advantage of it for business as well as sanity's sake. Your little ones will be happy to have another set of walls, different caregivers, and new playmates.

Keeping in touch while you travel

As a writer with my share of press trips and publicity tours under my belt, I understand the frustrations and challenges presented by hitting the road and leaving your kids behind. Not only must you deal with the stress of making trip and childcare preparations before you go, you must often make heroic efforts to keep in touch with the kids while you're traveling. Work and flight schedules often make this a virtual impossibility. There are a few solutions I've found that alleviate my kids' separation anxiety, reduce *my* anxiety, and make my trips less stressful and more productive:

- I leave a detailed itinerary—not just for the purposes of contact in case of an emergency, but so that my sons will know where I am, what I am doing, and will feel more a *part* of my life, even though they're not with me. When possible I leave them with information—travel brochures or guidebooks—about the place I'm going.

- I leave notes for my sons to read (or have the sitter read to them) for each day that I'm gone.

- I always send postcards. Even though they don't always arrive before I return home, the boys enjoy getting the mail and seeing where Mommy went.

- I sometimes leave a cassette tape of favorite bedtime stories or even just special messages. ("I'll be thinking of you today, wondering whether you won your soccer game.")

- I often leave them with a notebook, a simple camera, or a cassette recorder—and ask them to document the days I'm away with stories, pictures, and messages so I can relive these moments upon my return.

- I schedule as many evening phone calls as possible—even if it's just a 10-minute chat before bedtime.

Easing the transition back to home base usually means letting a suitcase sit or planning a take-out meal that first night or two back home. I often have a pile of mail and dozens of phone messages, but I wait until the kids are at school the next day before I dig in.

Running business errands

What do you do when you have a string of business errands you must run, but you also have the kids in your care? Short of hiring a sitter or saving errands until your spouse gets home, your best bet is to aim for one-stop shopping.

More and more shopping centers, even grocery stores, are offering an array of services all under the same roof. So instead of taking your kids in and out of their car seats while you visit the bank, the post office, the copy center, and the grocery store, go to those places where conveniences are available under one roof. For me, that's my local supermarket, which offers not only food and a pharmacy, but a bank, fax machine, copier, film developing, and package express service, not to mention a supervised children's play area. I can purchase a roll of stamps there and mail my letters, too.

Sometimes it's a matter of grouping these errands together. Drive-thru service is another godsend for any parent with young children. Where I live, I take advantage of the bank, dry cleaning, and fast-food drive-thru whenever possible, especially in inclement weather.

Another option is to run your errands when others are least likely to run theirs. Do your grocery shopping on Tuesday mornings while the rest of the world waits in line on Saturdays. Avoid the bank on Fridays or on the first or last day of the month. In essence, use your flexibility to your best advantage, both personally and for business.

Easy activities for the little ones

My neighbor Cindy is never at a loss for fun-filled activities, party games, and crafts for her kids. She readily plans inventive birthday party games and entertains a backyard full of kids, taking on the role of neighborhood mom. I, on the other hand, need to research such things in a book, or at the very least, spend significant cerebral energy in pursuit of such ideas!

But I have done my homework, and I'm ready to offer quite a few suggestions for keeping children entertained, educated, and occupied while work-at-home parents attend to business throughout the day.

Most work-at-home parents will tell you that keeping kids entertained and occupied is a neverending challenge, no matter how many books, crafts, or toys surround them. The rest of this chapter's activities run the gamut. Some may require your assistance, or a minimal amount of setup. Others might be left until a time when you can supervise the craft (unless you don't mind glue all over your kitchen!). Still others may appeal to your child if he or she is old enough to work a little more autonomously.

Before long your little ones will outgrow the need for preplanned amusements, and they'll be able to create their own play world without your assistance, and take the role of "entertainment coordinator" off your shoulders.

Extracurricular activities

In some families, the calendar is packed with soccer practice, Cub Scout or Brownie meetings, dance classes and recitals, music lessons, marching band, and the list goes on. In addition to keeping your kids busy while you work, such activities help children develop important social skills, team cooperation, and passions for hobbies that may last a lifetime.

However, parents should avoid packing their kids' agendas with so much structured activity that they leave little free time for creative play, personal hobbies, or unstructured amusements, says psychologist Dr. Kevin Leman. "We really need to slow down this process and let children have childhoods," Leman told me. "We're having them involved in too many activities. I'm on record as saying, get them out of those activities. Limit it to one or two."

Reading readiness

A good friend of mine who works at a bookstore, organizes wonderful events that introduce children to books and crafts. If there is an interactive bookstore in your area, stop in and learn how to recreate crafts at home on your own.

You can help build your child's reading skills and interest even *before* he or she is old enough to read. Once your child learns to read, this ability will offer countless hours of entertainment and adventure.

Toddlers can frequent storytime at the library where the librarian fosters the love of literature for short time periods. While you may be required to be nearby, you can be completing research or reading of your own.

Turn to television—in moderation

Certainly during the daytime hours, there are significant blocks of shows and cartoons perfect for entertaining and even educating young children. But the TV should be used in moderation—and *never* as an all-day baby sitter. You might consider scheduling TV time for your child to enjoy a favorite show—perhaps a half-hour before naptime or after lunch, or pop in a favorite video on occasion.

To avoid TV abuse, be sure that you monitor its use. Be familiar with the shows your children watch. Don't permit them to "channel-surf" or watch shows that aren't age-appropriate. Understand, too, that children cannot self-regulate their television use. It's up to *you* to announce that TV time is up and it's time to go outside or read or engage in some other activity.

How much TV is too much TV?

Years ago, I asked this question to TV's Fred Rogers. "Every child is different," he replied. "Some children can tolerate that kind of passive intake more than others, but all children need time for creative play, whether that means building, dressing up, or playing with siblings or friends. Television can never be a substitute for sociodramatic play."

Mr. Rogers went on to explain that even a shoebox could become a child's trolley, and that it's important to allow youngsters to play with whatever you have on hand. He suggested that kind of play is the basis of all adult problem-solving.

Time spent in front of video games, television, or even computers is time taken away from books, games, or vigorous exercise, which all children need.

It's important for parents to set good examples, too. If, every evening you sit down and let the TV hypnotize you until bedtime, you shouldn't be surprised if you struggle to drag your kids away from their favorite cartoons. If you're in the habit of keeping the set on all day "for company," your children will have a similar intimate relationship with the television.

High-, mid-, and low-tech alternatives to television

- Build a library of educational videotapes. Shows like *Sesame Street, Mister Rogers' Neighborhood, Shining Time Station, Barney & Friends,* and *Lamb Chop's Play Along* (PBS), and *Cappelli & Company* (Hearst TV stations), are great programs with educational, social, and entertainment value for preschool children. *Ghostwriter* and *Reading Rainbow* (both on PBS) are created for early elementary-age children. Nickelodeon's *Nick News, Bill Nye the Science Guy* (PBS), and *Where In the World Is Carmen Sandiego?* (PBS) are educational resources for children in grades 4 through 6.

- Many publishing houses are putting books and educational products together in packages to create hours of discovery and fun. Workman Publishing has been one of the pioneers with *The Bones Book, The Garden Book,* and *The Kids' Book of Chess.* With Workman, a jump rope, marbles, a kaleidoscope, etc., comes packaged with a book to read and the toy to experiment and practice with. Barron's has *Gardening Wizardry for Kids,* Running Press produces *The Holy Land Treasure Chest,* and Dorling Kindersley Publishing offers several different editions of its *First Activity Pack* for travel fun, world explorers, young detectives and scientists.

- If you do not need your computer all the time, grant access to your children so they can try some of the many educational software products. In fact, my Macintosh came with software my oldest son fell in love with—Broderbund's *The Amazing Writing Machine, The Oregon Trail, Grolier's Encyclopedia,* and the *American Heritage Children's Dictionary.* Workman's popular *Brain Quest* cards are available on diskettes and CD-ROM, and have won the Parents' Choice Seal of Approval.

- Microsoft offers series of educational software such as *Creative Writer II*, which offer wonderful ways to stretch your child's imagination and creativity. While designed with kids in mind, there's no reason parents can't take advantage of the clip art, writing and picture tools, Web page assistance, and e-mail capabilities.

- You'll find various encyclopedia editions available for the home and business computer. These avoid time-consuming trips to the library. Microsoft has the new *Encarta 97 Encyclopedia Deluxe Edition* for both Windows and Macintosh users. Parents and children will reap the benefits of thousands of articles, photos, and illustrations, video clips, animated sequences, and interactive features that can be used for business research or homework projects. Encarta offers World Wide Web links and free online updates that keep your information on the leading edge.

- Microsoft also produces software based upon the popular children's books and television show titled *The Magic School Bus.* Your kids will enjoy the incredible scientific field trips they can take right along with Ms. Frizzle and her class as they explore the age of the dinosaurs, venture inside the human body, visit a tropical rain forest, or dive the depths of the oceans.

- Foreign language comes alive on audio and videotapes, as well as CD-ROM, produced by Penton Overseas, Inc. *Lyric Language* is one successful program introducing languages to children through music and bilingual lyrics, using popular cartoon characters. For a brochure of Penton's products, call 800-748-5804.

- For something truly unique and brand-new, order your own edition of *It's News to Me,* a board game designed to encourage interest and participation in reading the newspaper. This game was introduced at the International Toy Fair in New York City, and was a part of the grand opening of the Newseum in Arlington, Va. Developed by Barbara Goldman of Newsline Publications, Inc., this game is geared for children ages 8 and up. (See the Resources section at the end of this chapter for ordering information.)

Games and other pastimes

"Mom, I'm bored!" If you've heard it once, you've heard it a million times, and unfortunately, you'll most likely hear it again! Next time your child says there's nothing to do, offer one or more of the following activities to keep him or her amused.

- Chess, checkers, or a word game such as Scrabble help kids develop their analytical and spelling skills.
- Jigsaw puzzles help develop patience and problem-solving.
- Duplo and Lego blocks stir the imagination and help little ones with their fine motor skills.
- Board games encourage siblings to interact, take turns, and learn how to play on fair terms.
- Computers are great tools for personal creativity and written expression. Encourage your child to do more than play video games, but to write thank-you notes, holiday newsletters, or special reports on their favorite topics.
- Turn clutter into collections. Encourage your youngsters to collect stamps, coins, leaves, sports cards...something they can be proud of and keep for themselves. An added bonus of this activity is that collecting teaches organizational skills and gives parents a peek into their child's world.
- Safety checks and supplies. Ask your older children to help you test such important devices as smoke and carbon monoxide detectors, flashlight batteries, earthquake kits, and first-aid supplies. If these items are lacking, allow your child to equip the device with new batteries, new emergency items, or whatever the case may be.
- Let them dress up in old clothes you keep in a fashion box.
- Line up your kitchen chairs and allow your little ones to play choo-choo train. Let them make tickets from construction paper, and keep an engineer's cap handy for pretend.
- Give your kids empty two-liter soda bottles, filled partially with sand to give them a little weight. Arrange these like bowling pins, hand them a soft (not heavy) ball, and let them bowl their hearts away!
- Save large cardboard boxes that new appliances come in (or ask around for them). Let your kids decorate them, play house, or build a fort.

When the phone rings

Your child may have ignored you all morning, content to draw, play games, or read. But as soon as that important client calls, your child will be under foot bouncing a ball, playing a musical instrument, asking for a snack, whining for attention, or presenting some other need that must be met *now*.

To counter this, keep a secret stash of surprises or snacks near the phone. Then when you get a call and your child suddenly appears, you can offer a forgotten toy or a healthy treat to distract him or her.

When you know in advance that you have an important call to make, pop in an engaging video. When I needed to be on the phone for a prescheduled radio interview that lasted longer than a half-hour, I taped several back-to-back episodes of my sons' favorite show. A virtual "Barney" brigade!

With a little luck, the novelty of the toys, the treats, or videos will entertain or occupy them so you can finish your call in peace.

How to be artsy when you're certainly not crafty

Whenever I try to illustrate anything for my sons, I'm reminded of why I'm a writer, not an artist! If you're like me, you know what it's like to strain yourself in order to be artsy-craftsy.

But after admiring the school crafts my children have brought home, and leafing through some books, I found it is possible to conceive fun-filled projects that we later hang with pride on our refrigerator or elsewhere in our home.

The most important factor for collaborating crafts at your kitchen table is collecting the right essentials—items you probably have on hand and are used to tossing in the trash or recycling bin. Keep these craft supplies in a central place where they are easy to grab when the urge strikes:

cardboard boxes	empty coffee cans	magic markers
Styrofoam trays	odd-shaped pasta	children's glue/paste
paper grocery bags	child-sized scissors	fabric scraps
old buttons	crayon pieces	old, odd socks
rick-rack, yarn	metal muffin tins	construction paper
craft sticks	old catalogs/magazines	

Try the following fairly simple projects to entertain your children when they're looking for fun and you desperately need a diversion!

Preschool crafts

- Make bag masks or sock puppets. Kids can cut holes for the eyes, draw faces, and make hair out of yarn, rick-rack, and glue. Sock puppets are simple to design with magic markers. When finished, the kids can plan a puppet performance.

- Create pasta doodles. Parents will have to cook, drain, cool, and separate the pasta, but once that's done kids can stick a picture or scene on dark colored construction paper. They can make flowers, houses, whatever they want. If they choose to preserve their creations, cover them with waxed paper and place a heavy book on top so they dry flat. The pasta should adhere. (Lasagna noodles can form the foundation of a house or a fire truck. Shell pasta makes the setting for a beach). You can use uncooked pasta to glue on to paper, but it's not nearly as flexible as it is when cooked.

- Turn a cardboard box into a car with a little help from construction paper, large buttons (wheels), fabric scraps (for the interior), and rick-rack or yarn (for details like bumpers, windows, and license plates).

- Build a food pyramid with pictures of food cut out from magazines or grocery circulars. Added bonus: Your kids will understand better next time you insist on a meal that's more than bread and sweets!

- Collect objects in coffee cans to form a keepsake collection (parents might want to sand any rough edges first). Hidden bonus: A couple of cans with plastic lids make great pretend drums.

Elementary-aged children's fun

- Kids love to play builder at the construction site. Your child can create a skyscraper or home, with a few craft sticks and children's glue. For variety, use various shapes including wooden meat skewers and tongue depressors.

- Create collections much the same way as collages, but have them organize the materials—leaves, shells, stamps or other items—and paste them on to clean Styrofoam meat trays.

- Salvage broken crayon pieces and place the remnants in a foil muffin tin or decorative craft pan and melt the remains in the oven until the different colors have blended together. Let cool, and now you have "crayon cookies" that even your preschoolers can color with for hours at a time. (Just make sure they're not eaten!)

- Let kids cut out photos from old magazines or catalogs to create hobby collages they can hang in their rooms. Paste the cut-out pictures on cardboard or a large sheet of paper. Not only will your children have loads of fun, but you'll gain insight into their favorite things.

Holiday or birthday gifts kids can make

Grandparents, aunts, and uncles already have their share of pictures and perfume, ties, and garden tools. A gift made by your children's own efforts will be remembered for a long time.

When the 50th anniversary of the Normandy invasion in France was approaching, my son Andy and I made some gifts for his Grandfather, with his World War II service in mind. We surprised him with an "army book" written just for him, complete with a poem, news magazine photos (it helped that *Time* and *Newsweek* ran cover stories), cutouts from catalogs depicting a soldier's life, and necessary gear. We pasted everything in a photo album and presented it for Father's Day that June.

Take into account your relative's or friend's interests, hobbies, or occupations. Or make something consumable (see page 149 in this chapter) or something simple as bath salts (using Epsom salts and perfumed oils).

Play dough recipe

Here's a great recipe for homemade play dough that your kids can use to sculpt to their heart's content. It's not meant to be eaten—but if it somehow *does* end up as a toddler's snack, there are no harmful ingredients.

2 cups flour	2 cups water
½ cup salt	2 tsp. cream of tartar
1 T. vegetable oil	drops food coloring

Mix over medium heat in large saucepan. Heat until ball forms. Remove from heat and cool for a few minutes until you can knead into large ball. Store it in an airtight container in the refrigerator and it should last several weeks or months.

Quick and easy finger paints

This recipe should definitely not be consumed!

½ cup cornstarch	one envelope unflavored instant gelatin
3 T. sugar	¼ cup mild liquid dishwashing soap
food coloring	water

Dissolve one envelope gelatin in ¼ cup hot water and let sit for 10 minutes. Combine cornstarch, sugar, and 1 ¾ cups cold water in a saucepan and stir until mixture is cloudy and smooth. Cook cornstarch mixture over medium heat on the stove, stirring occasionally until it's thick. Reduce heat. Add the gelatin mixture and dishwashing liquid. Stir again until smooth. Let cool.

Divide equal parts of the mixture into small bowls or airtight jars (if you want to use paints later). Add several drops of different food coloring to each container. Tip: Light colors are easiest to clean!

Kids can use these finger paints on newspaper surfaces, or even in the bathtub to create their own masterpieces.

Recipes kids can try

Everyone has to eat. Whether it's snack foods for around the house or on a trip, lunch box treats, or food gifts you give to friends and family, try these recipes that will keep your kids entertained in the kitchen!

Homemade granola

1 T. vanilla extract	¾ cup flaked coconut
½ cup vegetable oil	¼ cup light brown sugar
1 cup walnuts	2 ½ cups uncooked old-fashioned oatmeal
2 t. cinnamon	2 cups raisins or dried cranberries
½ cup honey	3 cups chocolate crisps cereal
¼ cup nonfat dry milk	

In a large bowl, mix dry ingredients, except raisins or cranberries. Combine oil, honey, and vanilla in a small saucepan and warm. Add to dry ingredients and stir until coated. Spread mixture evenly on a greased baking sheet. Bake at 300° for 30 minutes, stirring occasionally until granola is golden brown. Cool on tray for 30 minutes. Stir in raisins or cranberries. Store in airtight container or empty coffee can. Makes 12 cups.

Hot cocoa mix

1 cup nonfat dry milk

1 cup instant coffee creamer

1 cup chocolate-flavored powdered mix (more if desired)

1 cup mini-marshmallows

Stir together and store in airtight container. Add 3 tablespoons of mix to a mug of hot water or milk. Stir and top with whipped cream if desired.

Homemade pizza dough

In large bowl, dissolve:

1 pkg. dry yeast	¾ cup lukewarm water

Then add:

2 T. vegetable oil	1 t. sugar
½ t. salt	

Stir ingredients together, then add:
2 ¼ cup flour

Knead dough for five minutes. Allow to rise at room temperature several hours until double in bulk. When ready to prepare, punch down dough. Spread and press into greased pizza pan. Bake at 450° for 10 to 15 minutes. If you wish to make a complete pizza, garnish with pizza sauce, mozzarella cheese, and toppings before baking.

Yummy cookies kids can decorate

In large bowl, mix together:

1 cup soft margarine	1 egg
½ cup sugar	3 t. vanilla extract

Stir together and then add:

3 cups flour	½ t. baking powder

Chill cookie dough for at least six hours or overnight. Roll and cut with favorite cookies cutters. Decorate with sprinkles, if desired, before baking or wait until after for icing. Place on ungreased cookie sheets and bake at 425° for five to seven minutes.

Other edible ideas

- String O-shaped cereal on a long strand of dental floss.
- Planning a trip? Decorate a shoe box. Then pack each child's lunch into the box, along with a napkin, thermos, or juice box, and anything else that's needed. When it comes time to eat in the car, the lap box helps each child prevent spills!
- Make bagel sandwiches, fruit and cheese kabobs (with chocolate sauce for dipping on the side), pita pockets filled with salad, or veggies with ranch dressing.
- Mexican munchables can be made with small flour tortillas, shredded cheese, parsley or cilantro. Fold the ingredients inside the tortilla and microwave 15 to 25 seconds each or until melted.
- Look on the boxes of cereal, or the advertising sections of your Sunday paper for new and different recipes for things you probably have on hand. Manufacturers always have innovative ways to make party mixes out of cereal, even pizza or desserts from refrigerated pastry dough.

"Me work too!"

If that's a familiar refrain from your little one, set up a workstation near yours, equipped with a child's desk or table and chair. It's certainly a better option than seeing your own office gear commandeered, perhaps broken.

- Give your child a toy phone and some paper, crayons, or pencils. A small box with some index cards or old business cards can become a make-believe Rolodex.

- As you go through the day's mail, pass the catalogs and junk mail to your child. He or she can go through mail like you do.

- Flashcards available in toy stores or bookstores (DK Publishing has some for preschoolers) are educational and fun to have at your child's desk.

- Give your child little tasks to do that help you—like licking stamps and taping envelopes.

Finding kids' play things

If you struggle to find backyard play equipment, toys, or other items, you don't have to tax your budget or dip into business funds. Comb your local newspaper classifieds or community classified guide (called the *Pennysaver* in many cities). People often sell used baby and backyard equipment, toys, and other items you may need. Garage sales and flea markets are also wonderful venues for discovering outgrown toys and equipment.

You might have good secondhand stores near you that specialize in the resale of swings, swimming pools, plastic picnic tables, sliding boards, and playhouses. Look in the yellow pages under Consignment or Resale. Or check out national chains like Play It Again Sports (new/used sports gear), Once Upon a Child (new/used clothing, equipment, and toys), Computer Renaissance (electronics/computers), or Music Go Round (musical instruments).

Resources

Rainy Days & Saturdays by Linda Hetzer (Workman).

Cooking with Justin by Justin Miller (Andrews and McMeel).

Mister Rogers Talks with Parents by Fred Rogers and Barry Head (Family Communications Inc.).

Mister Rogers' Plan & Play Book: Daily Activities from Mister Rogers' Neighborhood (Family Communications, Inc.).

What to Expect, the Toddler Years by Arlene Eisenberg, Heidi E. Murkoff, and Sandee E. Hathaway, B.S.N. (Workman).

Bringing Up Kids Without Tearing Them Down by Dr. Kevin Leman (Thomas Nelson).

365 Afterschool Activities by Sheila Ellison and Judith Gray (Sourcebooks).

365 TV-Free Activities You Can Do with Your Child by Steve and Ruth Bennett (Adams).

The Rainy Day Activity Book by Jennifer Rader and Brian Foote (Main Street/Doubleday).

The Bones & Skeleton Game Book by Karen C. Anderson and Stephen Cumbaa (Workman).

1,400 Things to Be Happy About for Kids! by Barbara Ann Kipfer and Paul Meisel (Kipfer & Meisel).

Kids Create! Art & Craft Experiences for 3 to 9 Year-Olds by Laurie Carlson (Williamson Publishing).

Kids Learn America! Bringing Geography to Life with People, Places & History by Patricia Gordon and Reed C. Snow (Williamson Publishing).

Playing Together: 101 Terrific Games and Activities that Children Ages 3-9 Can Do Together by Wendy Smolen (Fireside).

Gardening Wizardry for Kids by L. Patricia Kite (Barron's).

Learn and Play In the Garden: Games, Crafts and Activities for Children by Meg Herd (Barron's).

It's News to Me board game by Barbara Goldman (Newsline Publications, Inc.).

Chapter 9

Involving your older children

It happened one day on a summer trip to my son's library. There, sitting with all the other moms and kids who had to recite their weekly book reports, my son Andy turned to a perfect stranger announcing, "My mom's an arfur." Pronunciation aside, I felt proud, validated by my 4-year-old, at the time.

However, this same child, three years later, turned to me in a moment of frustration, and said, "Why don't you get a job?"

Through these interactions, I learned that children don't just learn about the working world, money management, and career responsibilities by osmosis. It's important to share information about your job on a regular basis. Your kids are never too young to learn something valuable about work and business activity.

I'd worked from home pretty much since Andy was born. But his comments made it quite evident that I needed to explain why I spent time at the keyboard, and how what I did with that time helped to provide for the family's material needs.

What better way to educate your children about the business world than by allowing them to experience your business firsthand? "Even when you work at home, kids are often fuzzy about the nature of your business," says Janet Bodnar, author of the syndicated column,

"Ask Dr. Tightwad," and senior editor of *Kiplinger's Personal Finance*. "If kids had a better appreciation for what you were doing, they also might be more accommodating and less inclined to interrupt."

In this chapter I hope you'll learn more about kids, the home workplace, and the money-management matters that go along with growing up and joining the business world.

Kids can come in handy!

A good friend of mine, Pam, began a home-based business creating events, special gifts, and interior design. She clearly knows what it's like to be pressed against a deadline and desperate for help. In those situations, she recalls how her children have pitched in at the last minute.

"My daughter Amanda has helped me produce material when she's come home from high school and seen the need. No questions asked," says Pam proudly. "I remember when I did customized gifts for a corporate client, over a hundred gifts, and Amanda, along with her friend, helped me wrap these as we got closer to the deadline."

Pam's older son Jeff, now in his early 20s, has helped load and unload her car, inflate dozens of balloons with a helium tank, and decorate for an on-site event. "When it's obvious I have a big job, they help," she says. "But as teenagers they have their own lives, and that's important. You need to remember that your business is your business. Your children aren't responsible for making it successful."

There are many pluses to involving your kids in your business. By hiring your children to work in your business, you:

- Instill a good work ethic.
- May inspire an entrepreneurial streak in your child.
- Help them understand what you do for a living.
- Provide an educational experience that supplements classroom learning.
- Help them earn additional money.
- Gain valuable tax advantages.

However, if you're considering hiring your kids, you'd better think about the downside, as well. With kids as employees, you may discover that:

- Family members can be unreliable.
- Family squabbles spill over into the workplace.
- Children try to pull rank when there are others who work for you also.
- Interest will wane when the novelty has worn off.

Involving your children in your work can be a very rewarding experience—a chance to spend quality, productive time together, and it can build ties that last for years to come. By anticipating problems and setting up expectations, you might be able to overcome any of the negative aspects of having your kids work for you.

If the arrangement works out beyond your wildest expectations (and this is possible), why not surprise your helper with small business cards made up on the photocopier or computer? Or with older kids, monetary rewards speak volumes. A raise, when one is deserved, says what words often cannot.

Finding age-appropriate tasks

Not all jobs are created equal, and the same goes for your child's abilities. There are some very mature children at 8 or 9, and there are older teens who may need to work harder to develop their skills.

Generally, children ages 7 to 9 can:

- Affix stamps.
- Open the mail.
- Sort or staple papers.
- Stuff and seal envelopes.
- Cut coupons or articles from the newspaper.

Children 10 and older can:

• Help solve problems (including computer woes!).

• Answer the telephone professionally.

• Glean articles from trade journals or business publications.

• Load or unload your car, van, or truck.

• Run simple business errands (providing they can drive).

• Type letters and file materials.

• Assist with mass mailings.

Tax advantages

There are a few steps you must take to justify claiming your kids as employees: You must keep good records, with the hours the children have put in, the tasks they have accomplished, and the money they have earned.

This means the work your kids do for you must be legitimate for your business. It also means employing your children for a reasonable length of time. Auditors will not readily believe that your 8-year-old worked a 20-hour week, in addition to his or her school schedule.

The wages earned must be on par with what you would pay any other employee to perform a similar task. Try to convince the IRS that your 8-year-old is worth $20 an hour to stuff envelopes, and you might as well plead your case to the *Guinness Book of World Records* while you're at it.

The advantages? Children under 18 are not currently required to pay Social Security taxes on their earnings. Also, their earned income must exceed a certain dollar limit before those wages are subject to federal income tax. Check current tax laws for the amount of this limit.

You *can* hire your child to work in your business. It's a savvy and legal way to take care of their allowance with the blessing of the IRS. Your children earn spending money or cash to stash in the bank, and you write off the expense, lowering net profits. In essence, you are moving money from one account to another, shifting income out of your tax bracket and into theirs.

Check with a tax advisor for further details, for there is paperwork you must file, and perhaps other taxes you need to withhold. As of this writing, if you pay your child $600 or more during the year, you must file either a 1099 or W-2 form, reporting that income to the IRS.

How a good parent can be a great boss

For starters, a work-at-home parent should not force or coerce a child into working. But gaining work experience has many benefits, not to mention the income derived, the experience earned, and the newfound appreciation the child may walk away with in regard to a parent's efforts.

Follow these tips on the job for a smoother transition from parent to professional mentor:

- Clearly define the job position or task that your child will need to accomplish.

- Give any necessary training or instruction, especially if you have a preferred way of completing a certain function. This alleviates the hard time parents often have in getting their children to take directions on the job.

- Start kids out on small assignments that require a limited commitment on both ends. That way, if you find your child is less enthusiastic than he or she had promised, or if the arrangement isn't working out as you had planned, you can cancel it without hard feelings.

- Set deadlines, even if you set artificial deadlines in the beginning, to ensure that work is completed in a timely manner. Again, should the arrangement not work out satisfactorily, you won't be stuck at the last minute with unfinished work.

- Solicit your child's opinion and input. Ask him or her how you might better solve a particular problem. Every employee wants to feel a sense of ownership and pride in their work, and your child is no different.

- Have your child report directly to some other employee (if you have one).

- Finally, reward good work with verbal compliments and prompt payment for a job well-done. Mutual satisfaction and good communication cement a favorable working relationship for the future.

Finding your children's hidden talents

What teenager doesn't appreciate a paycheck? Indeed, monetary remuneration is a powerful incentive when it comes to kids helping in your home-based business. But there are other substantial rewards, and one of them is discovering their talents and utilizing them in a productive way.

When my friend Pam acquired an additional gift basket business, she hired her daughter again to help with the overwhelming amount of Christmas orders. She knew Amanda possessed musical abilities, but Pam found she had other artistic talents as well—good design suggestions that came in handy.

If you think back to your own early years in the workforce, it was a time of discovery as you undertook different jobs, succeeding at some, failing at others. In the end you eliminated some potential career paths, recognized skills you needed to build, and were thrilled with the validation you received for those skills you excelled at.

That's why showing your child various aspects of your business is so essential—not just for you, but for the child's benefit. Offer a taste of all aspects of the work world—bookkeeping and office work, customer service, and creative projects. Take your child with you as you visit the bank to deposit receivables, the post office to mail bills, and the printer to pick up marketing materials. Explain each errand in terms of why and how you do the things you do.

In your business discussions, check to see what things might sound like from your child's perspective. For instance, if kids only hear you complain about late-paying clients or overwork, they might surmise that your business is less fulfilling than it really is. Show the other side—the joy that comes from helping a client achieve success, a well-satisfied customer who loves your product, or the solutions that have come about after painstaking work, trial and error.

"Finding the right task is a matter of knowing your child," says Janet Bodnar. "If your child is a computer whiz, she would be great at working with your office equipment, installing software and showing you how to use it. If he has a gregarious personality, he might enjoy answering the phones. An artistically-inclined child could help design business cards or stationery."

Teaching children about money

Just as babies don't come from storks, money doesn't grow on trees. Yet the two concerns have a lot in common. Parents don't like to talk about either of them. Learning to manage money is a part of the maturing process as youngsters take on additional responsibility. With a little guidance, work-at-home parents can contribute to this learning process, teaching lessons that can last a lifetime.

Introduce children to the concept of money as early as possible. Teach counting by using stacks of coins, starting with 100 pennies, advancing to dimes, next onto nickels and, finally, as the years go by, dollars. Once the child has mastered each counting exercise, plan an outing to the store and allow him or her to spend the money on some favored item.

Decide early on whether you will give allowances. Some families believe money should be earned, since this is the way the world works. If that's your philosophy, use this chapter to find age-appropriate jobs for your children. Then reward a job well-done with money and praise. Children need to learn that work is beneficial in non-monetary ways as well.

Visit your bank with your children. Explain how you have a checking account for day-to-day use, and a savings account for larger, more meaningful purchases and investments. When you return home, set up a similar model for your child—a piggy bank for petty cash, one for savings, and a bank account for camp or college.

If your children are old enough to understand the concept of retirement, you might even want to set up an **Individual Retirement Account (IRA)** into which you place a portion of their earned income.

Discourage spending before earning. This promotes laziness and encourages spending beyond one's means.

Set aside a portion for charitable giving. This encourages a valuable form of responsibility—looking out for others.

Teach your child how to avoid impulse buying. Never give into a whining plea for the item of the moment. Instead encourage youngsters to think about their purchases ahead of time. Never let them walk into the store with jingling pockets searching for ways to spend their money. This sets up poor spending habits.

Visit a toy store and purchase games for your children that will allow them to face financial decisions in a playful way.

Involve older children in family budget talks and planning for college. Guide them in the use of their funds from part-time jobs, gifts, or inheritances. As psychologist Dr. Kevin Leman once told me, "I'm on record as calling this the "gimme" generation. We need ways of making kids more fully aware of what families are all about. So let your kids pay the bills at 11 or 12 years old. You sign them, of course, but let the kids write the checks."

Instill a sense of home economics. Encourage kids to clip coupons, read product labels, and compare prices. Comparison-shopping for smaller items teaches big lessons for major purchases ahead.

Set a good example. Says Janet Bodnar, "Even if you never say anything to your children about money, they will soak up your behavior like a sponge. So don't do anything you wouldn't want them to do—like running up big credit card bills."

Don't treat financial issues as if they were a dirty secret. Bodnar continues, "Talk about family finances in an age-appropriate and matter-of-fact way. You don't have to tell your kids how much you make. But with young children, for example, you could talk about how the money you take out of the bank machine got there in the first place. Kids 10 or 11 are old enough to participate in discussions about what kind of car to buy or where to go on vacation (and save for it, too!)."

Discuss advertising come-ons. Once you know what's being beamed at your children, explain that advertising is how companies try to get you to spend your money. Ask why that famous football star might be pitching a soft drink? Is he being paid to? What if he can't even stand the stuff? Putting a realistic spin on the glitz of advertising often brings it down to a level where kids can understand the money behind the message.

Give your children a discretionary slush fund. Whether it's part of their allowance, or a portion of the money they earn from helping you in your business, they're going to need money in order to learn money management. That means watching them blow it occasionally on candy or some other frivolous item, but as long as the purchase doesn't violate family values, let them squander a portion. With any luck they'll learn better for next time!

Teaching business etiquette

Even if your children have no interest or inclination to work for you, at least teach them some basic business etiquette—particularly in terms of answering the phone. If you have a separate business line and an answering machine, the rules may be as simple as "Don't ever pick up my business line."

If your phone is for business and home, or your kids are older, it's probably wise to train them on proper phone-answering and message-taking techniques. You'll probably want them to answer with the name of your business, rather than the informal "Hello," they may be used to. Then, if you're not available, instruct them on how to take detailed messages (writing them down instead of committing them to memory), capturing at least the name, phone number, and time of call. If your kids check the answering machine for messages, instruct them to save messages on the machine until you hear them.

As for teaching sound business principles, the best method is to model good business behavior. Treat clients and customers courteously, reign in any complaints, or simply keep them to yourself. Show dedication to your work. Even if you work late at night in your pajamas, or get up early with a cup of coffee, kids pick up on parents' behavior. Of course, good communication fosters the best understanding. As I learned from my experiences, I need to speak of the work I do more often, lest my children think I'm playing computer games all day!

What if my child doesn't want to work for *me?*

Many work-at-home parents hope that their children might be infected with the entrepreneur bug, and get involved in the business. Children often have their own plans. Although they may be eager to work, they may not be interested in your business.

My guess is that if a child is eager to work, money is an important motivating factor. And why not? Money is how we obtain most anything we need or want. But while your child is motivated by dollar signs, try to see some of the other benefits their work will bring them—independence, decision-making abilities, self-confidence that builds through continual success, even lessons learned from on-the-job failures. If that means going to work for *another* entrepreneur—or even starting their own business—that's good, too.

The best book I've seen on the subject of young entrepreneurship is called *Fast Cash for Kids* by Bonnie and Noel Drew (Career Press).

In a sense, it's similar to this book you're reading, with ideas on ventures and important issues you need to think about, but it's written for the children. Try getting a copy of this book for your child to read, and others that give more specific information on beginning a successful part-time business.

Encourage your child's decision to pursue an entrepreneurial venture or a job with someone else. The lessons they'll learn are much more valuable than simply the money they'll earn. With their job will come financial responsibility and some purchasing freedom. Sure they could have learned these lessons from your home business, but the important thing is that your child is eager to work and earn money. Give this responsible step your blessing.

Resources

Dr. Tightwad's Money-Smart Kids by Janet Bodnar (Kiplinger).

Dear Babysitter by Vicki Lansky (Meadowbrook Press).

Mom, Can I Have That? Dr. Tightwad Answers Your Kids' Questions About Money by Janet Bodnar (Kiplinger).

The ABC's of Business by Dr. Cynthia Iannarelli and Jodi-Lynn Iannarelli, with Pamela Brooks (children's book, 800-NECWB-4-U).

Capitalism for Kids by Karl Hess (Enterprise Publishing).

A Small Business Guide to Employee Selection by Lin Grensing (Self-Counsel Press).

Hiring the Best by Ann M. Magill (Irwin Professional Publishing).

The Kid's Money Book by Neale S. Godfrey (Macmillan).

Fast Cash for Kids by Bonnie and Noel Drew (Career Press).

Employees: How to Find and Pay Them, a booklet from the U.S. Small Business Administration (SBA Publications, 800-827-5722).

Making Cents: Every Kid's Guide to Money by Elizabeth Wilkinson (Little, Brown & Co.).

Chapter 10

Redefining yourself

Broadcast the fact that you work at home to friends and neighbors, and you just might be the most popular person on the block. You'll be the one they call when they need someone to pick up their mail, to lend a listening ear or a helping hand, or to watch the kids at the bus stop because all the other parents "work." Most businesspeople who work at home agree that perception becomes a problem. Somehow a home-based business isn't always taken as seriously as it should be. So at the outset, let me make one important point. Take yourself seriously, for if you don't, no one else will.

Whenever we make a significant change, such as working from home, its impact is felt in all aspects of our lives. Even when the change is for the better, it can sometimes leave us uncertain and a little frightened. As we venture forth to build and develop our new business and nurture our families, we're having to deal with a new identity. That's what this chapter is about. It addresses those issues that come into play as we define our new career and role as an at-home parent. It touches on issues such as others' perceptions of our professionalism, the importance of setting up support systems, the impact this change may have on our marriages and our professional relationships, and more. Perhaps most importantly, it focuses on defining ourselves beyond our work persona and parental role.

Wait a minute...I work!

Imagine your indignation if you overheard people talking about you, and they said "Sally doesn't work. She just stays home."

Unfortunately, some may look at your endeavors as a nice little hobby you have going. It might be looked upon as busywork that's inconsequential, done for pin money. Others may think you work from home out of desperation because you couldn't find any other type of employment. Most unfortunate is the attitude some vendors might harbor that any monies owed to you can wait. It's not urgent. After all, it's only a supplemental income.

You get used to hearing stereotypes, and one tactic I've used is to write off those stupid comments as ignorance. Anyone with an ounce of business savvy knows that work-at-home businesses are the wave of the future, but there are strategies you can use to improve your perception in the minds of others.

- Avoid seeing clients at your home office. Meet them at another location away from children, pets, and daily living.

- Keep a blazer handy in your car when you're running business errands. I'll never forget standing in the photocopier line at my local office store when a very pushy woman (in her suited business attire) made it clear to the others that her work took priority, for it was W-O-R-K. I guess she thought the rest of us were simply there to chat!

- Carry a briefcase on errands and when you go out on business appointments.

- If you have pets, have a lint brush handy for last-minute clothing cleanup.

- Print business cards. You'd be surprised how 500 pieces of rectangular card stock can raise your credibility quotient. When people look at your card, they get a split-second image of what you're all about. Your cards must correspond to the image you want to portray. Therefore, use one typography style, varying this with boldface, embossing or creative spacing. Remember to print your phone number at the top, and leave room at the bottom to accommodate a Rolodex.

- Add a second phone line that's used exclusively for business calls. Instruct your children how to answer a call and take a message, or ask them not to answer the telephone during certain hours of the day.

- Manipulate your address. If your street address does not sound professional enough, you can always have an address of your choice at your local mailing store. A post office box might also suffice. If you live in an apartment building, use the word suite instead of apartment.

- Project a vibrant appearance. It might be difficult when you're juggling children and running business errands with them in tow to appear is if you're never frazzled but give it your best shot. A deep breath and a smile can help!

- When you're not working solo, wear professional attire. Remember the old rule of dressing for the job you want, not the one you have? Now that you have the job you've always desired, don't jeopardize your image with sloppy appearance. Books on finding the right styles and colors to enhance your wardrobe are readily available. Image consultants can lend a hand and often tip the scales in your favor.

- If you want your business to appear larger than it actually is, eliminate signs of smallness. People's first impressions are often formed by the telephone. If calls go unanswered, if callers get a busy signal, or if there's an inappropriate message or background noise, your operation suggests you are less serious than your competitors. Voice mail, available through the telephone company, allows you to have every call answered.

Facing subtle put-downs

What's most important is that you respect your decision to work from home as a career and lifestyle choice, and one that was initiated with your children's best interests in mind.

Remember, most rude, stereotypical remarks are rooted in ignorance, and sometimes repressed jealousy. But I'll give you some ammunition, or simple reassurance, that you (and your children) are indeed gaining much more than you are sacrificing.

Dr. Kevin Leman is one of my favorite parenting authors and a frequent guest on national talk shows such as *Good Morning America.* I especially like his ability to cut to the quick of things, in this case, the need for nurturing young children.

In his book *Bringing Up Kids Without Tearing Them Down,* Leman writes, "As much as I sympathize with moms who have to work—especially single moms, who seldom have any other choice—I still come down on the side of having parents do everything they can to keep at least one parent home as the key caregiver for children through grade school, and preferably well into high school. And, if at all possible, this person should be the mother."

Leman goes on to applaud fathers who make career sacrifices in order to parent their children, and he supports his statements with research regarding the psychological imprinting of young children. He's careful to add that he doesn't want to place a guilt trip on working mothers, but his book does encourage families to explore every option available to them, including working from home. "The advantages are obvious: You're close to your kids, you avoid the commuter hassle, your hours can be flexible, and if you are in business for yourself, your overhead should be very low," says Leman.

Other parenting authorities are the authors of the popular book *What to Expect—the Toddler Years.* These women suggest taking the offensive when defending your decision to stay at home. As they write, "When a listener nevertheless responds condescendingly, you can again turn the tables: 'I know this isn't for everyone. Not everyone can be a good parent—it takes a lot of smarts, good instincts, ingenuity. It's the toughest job around—but also the most rewarding.' " Work-at-home professionals merely need to add the part about how rewarding a home-based business can be.

Furthermore, you can offer something like "I'm always up to new challenges. This one might be one less chosen, but it adds to my life and career tremendously."

Next time you feel left out of the corporate climb or the nine-to-five routine, remember why you're working from home, and realize that if you had a more traditional career and schedule, you'd probably be yearning for what you have now. It matters more what you believe than what you can communicate to others who question your decision.

So you're expecting?

Unfortunately, it might be best to delay imparting the news of your pregnancy to clients or customers. When I was expecting my oldest son, I did encounter those who seemed to believe that once a woman's abdomen grew, her brain shrunk!

Hopefully you won't encounter such notions, but it's wise to wait until your second trimester before announcing that you are expecting. Of course, if you are showing early or if complications arise, you might not have a choice. Postponing the news gives you time to create contingency plans, because every client or customer will wonder about the business or project you're involved in. Be prepared to answer questions such as "Will you quit?" or "How long will you be gone?"

When you do share your delight with them, still guard against sharing too many details of your physical condition or nursery color scheme. It's wise to keep things on a business level, unless you know that such discussions won't weaken your position. Invest in professional maternity clothing, and don't let people's archaic attitudes daunt you. Many women have combined careers, home-based businesses, and motherhood.

Finding help while you're away

Sooner or later in most home businesses, the proprietor will suddenly realize he or she needs a break. Worse yet, a medical crisis or family emergency forces the question when they are least prepared.

Make contingency plans now for how you'll run your business should you become ill, have to care for one of your children, or simply need a vacation with the family. Is there another member of your family, close friend, or colleague who could help you out in a pinch?

Say you're an events planner with a scheduled news conference. Much of the work is done, but since your 6-year-old just came down with chicken pox, you won't be able to attend the event. Here's where having a colleague who has handled such details pays off. Maybe she's another self-employed professional. Maybe he's out of the business, but can call upon the experiences of years past. Experience counts. If an emergency comes your way, you want to turn your client's affairs over to someone who is up to the responsibility.

In another case, you might need a break. By letting clients know your plans in advance, you can usually arrange major projects around your schedule. You might worry about their reactions, but most will likely say, "Have a great time."

In the case of maternity or paternity leave, or some other short-term disability, work ahead as best as you can. That's what I did while pregnant with my second son. Wouldn't you know, he arrived three months early! Fortunately, the project I was working on at the time, my book *Writing for Money,* was nearly completed except for a few quotes and paragraphs.

If you need to hire temporary help in the form of an equally capable colleague, friend, or family member, make sure he or she has access to your office and files, and knows how to reach you at all times. When you return, check with your clients or customers, letting them know they're still a priority and you appreciate their understanding.

Moving your business

You're settled into your profitable home-based business when your spouse suddenly calls with the exciting news of a corporate transfer to another city. Well, if you read earlier sections in this book on conquering clutter, you could reframe this dilemma as a good opportunity! But I understand the concern. For a brief moment I experienced the idea of relocation, and moving my business was definitely a concern.

If you have a choice in where you move, take a look at past issues of *Home Office Computing* or *Money* for their ranking on the best cities for entrepreneurs or small businesses. Also investigate with the local chamber of commerce to see if there are support organizations for home-based entrepreneurs. In my hometown of Pittsburgh (which ranked fourth in the *Home Office Computing* survey in 1995), we're fortunate to have the Small Business Development Center at Duquesne University. This group works as a confidential clearinghouse for people with questions. It conducts biannual zoning surveys of the area townships, and annually hosts a conference which attracts noted speakers and experts to share their thoughts on home businesses.

You can also seek advice through various Internet newsgroups and message boards. Post that you're looking for advice, and I'll bet you receive a few helpful responses.

Besides the research you can do, prioritize your tasks. When you work from home, the implications for moving are particularly harrowing. You're also moving a family, and you'll need to conserve your energy for all the adjustments bound to occur. Determine what tasks have to be accomplished soon, and gradually set aside time after that to establish your home office, your local networking and support services, and seek new clients.

Just as you might pack a special "open me first" box filled with household necessities (like light bulbs, cleaning supplies, toilet paper, soap, and coffee pot), you'll want to do the same for your office. In this survival kit, include stamps, stationery and envelopes, business cards, important ongoing files you'll need, important records, and your Rolodex. In fact, you might want to personally carry a box like this in your car if you're driving to your new home. Otherwise, label it carefully for the moving truck.

Moving your business is most definitely a challenge, but you may find that it opens up new doors for marketing your business, and results in a better bottom line in the years ahead.

Why the marital spats?

Many a work-at-home parent has had to make marital adjustments based upon their businesses. One doesn't have to be a therapist to figure out the causes of the tension. It's likely that everyone's expectations were inflated. Frequently we trade everyday hassles when we work from home. Instead of scraping snow off the car or waiting for the train, we sigh at leftover dishes, or see our spouse making "just one more call" from our home office phone.

"During the time of the parenting imperative—those very crucial years when the needs of the children tend to take precedence over those of the adults in the family—most research shows that couples find their marriage less satisfying," reports Carol M. Anderson, Ph.D., of the University of Pittsburgh Medical Center. Dr. Anderson, a family therapist and marriage counselor, also says that couples shouldn't worry if they occasionally squabble. "But if the fights never end, or if the children are drawn into the middle of them and forced to take sides, if one or both partners is consistently psychologically removed or terminally bored, it's worth getting worried."

Money matters

It's a shame that financial gain seems to validate what we do in our professional lives, for we so often base our success upon our net worth. By now I hope you see that I identify with the financial struggles of some work-at-home parents.

A very good friend, whom I know has my best interests at heart, casually asked one day, "If you add up the hours you put in, how much do you think you make on an hourly basis?" I have to admit that between the lines of that question, I perceived the hidden thought of "come on, can you really make any money working from home?"

Also distressing was the husband on the other side of divorce litigation who referred to my home-based career as "this hobby I work at," and in my mind, seemed to ridicule my lowered earning capacity.

I have to reply that I'm proud of what I do. No amount of money can replace the value I receive and I believe my children benefit from when they see me meeting their needs, both maternally and materially. (With young children, you may find you don't earn quite as much money as home-based workers with self-sufficient teenagers.)

As for adding up hours, the self-employed professional might not always net the same hourly amount on each job. Some tasks will be a snap, making the job very profitable. Others that require more effort (but provide intangible benefits like learning or future contacts) net you less. If you are disciplined and hard-working, opportunities will come your way, and the income will follow in proportion. What you earn today is not necessarily what you will earn tomorrow.

Another friend of mine ran a communications business from her home, prior to adopting a baby boy. I asked her recently how she made the transition from working at home without children, to working with one. "It's all worth it. I love being a mom," Nanette says. "I think it was a major adjustment, but one for which I felt pretty prepared. I do miss the sense of accomplishment from being able to become fully immersed in work." Once again, only a small sacrifice.

Parents who feel good about themselves have more to give their children. Enjoy your work, relish in the fact that it reaches out to other people and professionals, and be proud that it makes your life—and your children's—that much better!

Better communication should be the first solution, whether privately or with the help of a qualified counselor. I've known couples who have been upfront about their fears and expectations, and others who couldn't voice the simplest concern. One home-based mom acknowledged that she thought her husband might pester her each week for what she'd billed to clients. A husband admitted to me that, at first, he wondered if his wife's home-based business might restrict him with future career opportunities he might want to pursue. And most couples reported a certain element of envy that crept into their relationships, with spouses wishing they could work from home as well—or envying the validation that a traditional office, secretary, staff, and regular paycheck offered.

Keep the lines of communication open. Find time to talk about pet peeves and hidden worries you've tucked away, for if you don't, they're sure to creep into other aspects of your marriage. And practice the art of switching mental gears—learning to physically and emotionally close the door to work when it's time to relax and make your children and your spouse a priority. That might mean saying no to additional work, but if it improves the quality of your life, the balance between work and family, and your marriage, that's perfectly okay. As my friend Nanette puts it, "For the first time in my life, I've had to say no a couple of times, which is very hard for me to do."

Does divorce affect a home-based business?

I can wholeheartedly relate to anyone's fear that separation or divorce will have consequences for his or her career. When my husband, after 11½ years of marriage, insisted we separate, I thought it might end my ability to work from home. He was the main provider, and I was the economically-dependent spouse. He helped with childcare, errands, and chores. How would I make it on my own?

With the separation I quickly realized that my marriage was not a healthy one, that there were behaviors I simply could not tolerate any longer, and that my original premise about my career and business demise was a quick judgment made of fear. I realized that time would be at a premium, and finances would indeed be tighter. I tried to focus on the positive outcomes.

For starters, a peaceful home is the best kind there is, certainly more conducive to productive work. And the children would be spending some time with their father, enabling me to concentrate on work without interruption. Visitation equaled childcare, without the out-of-pocket expense. Legally, my husband was required to pay child and spousal support. I found that I had fewer roles in my life. The time I had spent seeing to his needs could now be spent with my children and building my business. Living apart spelled relief from additional cleaning, laundry, grocery shopping, and meal preparation.

If you feel separation and divorce are imminent, take the necessary steps to protect yourself, your children, and your home-based business. That spouse who promises not to squabble over little things or cause trouble in some way invariably does. It's simply a complication of divorce that things get uglier before they get better.

Seek legal advice. Transfer funds into your own name and establish your own credit. Find all pertinent business and tax records, proof of bank accounts and investments, pension plans and social security records, and keep these in a safe place.

File immediately for child and/or spousal support. Do not just take the word of the spouse who promises to provide for whatever you need. File, and you'll have an official court order for support and the enforcement that goes along with failure to comply.

Document the dates and amounts you have spent on childcare. I was amazed when a recent court hearing limited the amount the court considered reasonable for my child-care expenses. For the economically dependent spouse, such views make it more difficult to expand your business. I know people looking for jobs who must use childcare to gain the time to improve their lot in life. It's a catch-22 situation, but the only way around it is to have good records and proof. Also, if you rely upon the children's other parent for childcare, be sure to have a back-up plan in place. I've had to use one several times when my ex failed to pick up the boys.

Sure there will be challenges. If taking a more traditional job with benefits and a steady paycheck is necessary, look for ways to continue your home business on the side or put it on hold for a while. But don't make quick decisions in the first few months following a separation or divorce. Don't automatically assume your home-based business is doomed. It could very well prosper as a result of your divorce!

12 tips for nurturing yourself

If you're ever so busy with managing your business, caring for the children, and seeing to everyday details, that you push aside the need to take care of yourself, take a minute to think of this: One of the key influences on children's development is the amount of stress in their families' lives. Here are 12 tips that hopefully you can use whenever the need arises:

- **Breathe deep.** The premise of aromatherapy is that the brain links how you feel with what you smell. Sip herbal tea or light a scented candle.

- **Explore new places.** Reserve a Saturday to check out a museum you've never been to, visit the library, or window shop. Do something a little unfamiliar as a treat to yourself.

- **Prevent burnout.** When someone asks you to take on a new commitment (social, volunteer, or otherwise), establish an "I'll have to get back to you" policy. This way, you're less likely to overextend yourself.

- **Eat well.** You've heard of "mood foods?" Well, it's true that we are what we consume, so try to limit junk food, sweets, and items that don't agree with you. Curb the caffeine. I know this is tough, but the temporary increase in alertness is usually followed by greater fatigue, and sometimes depression. Increase the amount of calcium-rich and whole-grain foods, fruits, and vegetables. If you crave carbohydrates (pasta, potatoes), go ahead and have a second helping. For women, carbohydrates can even alleviate premenstrual symptoms and mood swings (vitamin therapy works for some women also).

- **Be crafty.** Try your hand at some creative outlet you've always wanted to do. Sculpting, needlepoint, woodworking, even writing. You'll learn something about the hobby, and maybe about yourself.

- **Get physical.** Jogging, brisk walking, tennis, golf, or racquetball helps you physically and mentally. Swimming, in particular, is excellent exercise with the added calm of the water.

- **Be friendly.** Whether you're kind to an absolute stranger, extend courtesy to someone in your family, or call a friend in a mini-crisis, friendliness goes far.

- **Delegate.** Learn to ask others for the help they'd probably be very willing or capable of offering. This means children can help carry the laundry basket and fold the contents, or your spouse can plan, shop, prepare, and clean up a meal. Things might not turn out exactly as they would had you completed the task, but you will have gained.

- **Daydream.** It's the equivalent of a mental vacation when you can't leave the house, let alone the country! Imagine yourself somewhere tropical, or before a roaring fire on a cold winter's night.
- **Laugh a little.** Humor lightens up the tension in yourself and those around you.
- **Listen to soothing sounds.** And lights and sensations. Whatever works for you to relax the spirit or the body, whether it be soft music, warm lights, or a neck massage, enjoy the pampering.
- **Be romantic.** Whether it's curling up with a good romance novel or making love with your partner, sex, or the thought of it, stimulates the body's release of endorphins (natural opiates that create a sense of euphoria and relieve pain).

Exiting one business, entering another

The experience I shared earlier in the book in regard to the newsletter I published leads me to discuss how one gracefully exits one business and enters another. About three years into publishing this newsletter, I realized I had a decision to make. I either had to devote a massive amount of time to educating my target audience about the benefits of this newsletter, or I could call this publishing effort a learning experience, and move on to something potentially more lucrative. When the contract for my book *Writing for Money* was offered around this same time, the decision was easy. I decided to move on.

Knowing your limitations might be part of the larger process of finding your calling in life. I'd never truly explored becoming an author, but it worked out to be the best decision I could have made. Don't worry about others thinking you have failed. If you frame the transition from one business venture into another properly, it will enhance your reputation, not detract from it. Too many people fail to pursue a dream, or dare to try their ideas in the marketplace. It's the rare person who has the courage to forge ahead. Whatever the outcome, something good transpires.

Still you want to exit gracefully, for someday you may need these clients or customers in your corner. Honor your existing commitments, if possible. In my case, I fulfilled all subscription orders. I then sent thank-you letters, explaining my new venture as an author, and promised to be in touch when the book was released. It's wise to notify the media as well. For my newsletter, that meant returning the paperwork to a directory in which my publication had been listed. In the next edition, it would be noted that I'd ceased publication.

Inform people, even if it means returning correspondence to the sender with a message of "refused/out of business." This conveys that you haven't exactly fallen off the earth. It's common courtesy that builds goodwill, and a potential following, for your next venture.

A new look for a new you

Few home-based workers think seriously about their wardrobe as a factor in their career success. Indeed, when I stopped working nine to five in the downtown atmosphere, few people saw me, outside of my son, neighbors, and delivery people. After Alex was born, I got out even less. So why should I care about clothing? Isn't this nonchalance the beauty of working from home?

Yes and no. Yes, in that it's great to be able to work some mornings or evenings in your pajamas and robe. As long as the work is accomplished, no one cares. But some of us simply feel better about ourselves if we know we look the part. Indeed, while I enjoy "jama work," there are also days when instead of changing out of a suit or dress and jacket after an appointment, I choose to keep it on, head for my desk, and continue to work. If you're like me, you'll find there are days where it's appropriate to dress down, and days when you must put on all the finishing touches.

John Molloy wrote the *Woman's Dress for Success Book* which first appeared in 1977. Twenty years later, we can rely upon the new edition of his reference where he writes, "Today the debate is not over whether women should dress for success, but how they should go about doing it."

What I liked about his book then and now is the advice he gives not only on wardrobe selection, but accessories, hairstyles, and more. You may not agree with what Molloy says, but he has done his research, and there's surely something every woman can learn from it.

For those times when wardrobe matters, you don't necessarily need to dress in a suit with stockings and high heels. But as a home worker, you should strive for comfortable clothing that can also identify you as professional, should you run business errands or otherwise

Sanity savers

Throughout this book, and particularly in this chapter, I've tried to give firsthand advice and expert insights on how to make a career work when raising a family at the same time. I'd like to reiterate a few thoughts to give you the added boost you will need as you go about the days and months ahead:

- **Ask for support in advance.** Don't be shy. If you need help, especially in the initial stages, simply explain your plan and solicit assistance. I've found that most people are very understanding, especially if you explain your circumstances, your goals, and your willingness to return a favor that you can provide (even if it's at a later date).

- **Ignore nay-sayers** or those who just don't get it. That means, if your banker turns you down for a small business loan, look elsewhere for financial backing. Don't give up. If your neighbor keeps dropping by to chat or calling you when you're trying to work, get tough (of course, in a polite way). This point ties into the preceding two.

- **Stay connected.** Even if you've left behind a corporate position or switched careers completely, it will probably be of great psychological value if you maintain ties with former co-workers. Schedule a lunch date. Attend professional organization meetings. Seek out new business groups that will give you a reason to get dressed up, out of the home office, and into the extended world of your fellow professionals. If all else fails, volunteer for a project that uses your talents and puts you into a new mix of people.

- **Speak confidently of what you do.** Even before a divorce, I think my husband took for granted how hard I worked on both the professional and personal fronts. If he didn't see it, I'm sure others did not focus on my workload either. So hear this, home workers! You have talents and skills. You should be proud of what you do and how hard you work. In fact, you have not only one job, but two, which you are managing concurrently. Tell that to the rest of the world. (If that doesn't work, give them their own copy of this book and tell them to write to me.)

Honesty, combined with drive, determination, an ounce of good humor, and at times a tough exterior, make the difference. These are all ingredients toward a better self-image, your own sanity (and your family's as well), and ultimately, your career's success.

encounter people in the course of your day. Even casual attire has influence. If the jeans are so tight that you can't breathe, maybe no one will notice by phone or fax, but you'll notice if the discomfort takes your mind off of work and onto more personal matters.

Periodically go through your closet and make sure your wardrobe fits well and works in today's business climate. Since many women combining businesses with child-rearing undergo body changes as a part of motherhood, the need is even greater. Give away or sell items that aren't serviceable any longer, and make it a point to shop for items that project the image of a successful entrepreneur. Jan Larkey's book *Flatter Your Figure* is a gift to those of us women who have undergone motherhood, lifestyle, and workplace changes. Larkey shows how to accent your assets and disguise the rest.

The kind of clothing and accessories you purchase is your decision based upon your circumstances. But at one time or another, each of us attends conferences, runs business errands, meets with a banker, or comes face to face with important contacts. Thus, I urge you to peruse the pages of these books, clear out wardrobe has-beens, and make room for new acquisitions. If nothing more, chalk it up to business preparation. Next time you must make an impression, you'll be ready.

Good things can happen to you

A lot of us buy into the belief that things happen for a reason. However, random events do occur, and I think the main difference that distinguishes successful people from the discontented is attitude as well as adjustment ability.

Attitude is everything, especially for parents who desire to blaze their own paths. If you exude confidence, it will become infectious. Your friends, romantic partners, children, customers, and clients will pick up on your happiness, and want to work with you, buy from you, and generally be near you.

Attitude also affects another reality—adjustment. While I know some of you reading this book have entered working at home with a preconceived plan, others struggle. Maybe you would just as soon work in a traditional office because you're fearful of the risks, but perhaps that sought-after corporate spot isn't anywhere to be found. Maybe you've always dreamed of leaving one type of work to engage in your real passion. There might be nay-sayers who are quick to dismiss your dreams. Maybe you feel stuck, financially bound to what pays the bills.

For all of these scenarios, I say "Take charge!" Reign in what's wrong in your life and don't hesitate to step away from it. Tomorrow can be drastically different than today. As Joan Lunden writes in her latest book, "What sets apart the winners of this world is that they put their thoughts into action instead of passively waiting around for things to change."

Resources

100 Ways to Motivate Yourself by Steve Chandler (Career Press)

You Are Special by Fred Rogers (Viking).

The Good Marriage by Judith S. Wallerstein and Sandra Blakeslee (Houghton Mifflin).

Inner Simplicity by Elaine St. James (Hyperion).

Getting the Love You Want: A Guide for Couples by Harville Hendrix, Ph.D. (Harper).

You Just Don't Understand: Women and Men In Conversation by Deborah Tannen, Ph.D. (Ballantine).

Men Are from Mars, Women Are from Venus by John Gray, Ph.D. (Harper Collins).

50 Ways to Keep Your Lover by Linda Thompson (Longstreet).

Recipes for Romance by Leslie and Jimmy Caplan (New World Library).

Having It All / Having Enough by Deborah Lee, Ph.D. (Amacom).

52 Ways to Reduce Stress In Your Life by Connie Neal (Thomas Nelson).

Joan Lunden's Healthy Living by Joan Lunden and Laura Morton (Crown).

Flying Solo by Carol M. Anderson and Susan Stewart, with Sona Dimidjian (Norton).

New Women's Dress for Success by John T. Molloy.

Flatter Your Figure by Jan Larkey (Simon & Schuster).

Inspiration to get you started

One Sunday at church, my minister, the Rev. Richard R. Ollinger, gave a sermon on faith, decisions, and how we use our time. It made me think of my own choices—how I choose to work at home so that I can be there for my children, but also how hard it is for others to act upon an idea or new venture.

I'd like to offer a portion of the sermon, with a poem, to validate the choices you've already made, or hopefully inspire you to make new ones.

Have you ever noticed that if dreams are not acted upon quickly, they very often fade away and eventually die? Some unknown person penned a poem with the simple title, Tomorrow, and it has food for thought:

He was going to be all that a mortal should be
No one would be kinder or braver than he
Tomorrow.
A friend who was troubled and weary he knew,
Who'd be glad of a lift, and who needed it, too;
On him he would call and see what he could do
Tomorrow.

Each morning he stacked up the letters he'd write
And thought of the folks he would fill with delight;
It was too bad, indeed, he was busy today,
And hadn't a minute to stop on his way;
More time he would have to give others, he'd say
Tomorrow.
The greatest of workers this man would have been;
The world would have known him had he ever seen
Tomorrow.
But the fact is, he died, and he faded from view,
And all that he left when his living was through
Was a mountain of things he intended to do
Tomorrow.

So many people have dreams and they never act upon them.
They grow accustomed to the way things are, and even though
they know things could be better, they lack the passion and the
faith to make their dreams come true, and soon those dreams
fade away.

Don't let your dreams fade away! Here's hoping these words of wisdom—and the rest of this book—have made a difference for you, your career, and your children!

—Loriann Hoff Oberlin

Resources for work-at-home parents

The following resources are listed to help work-at-home parents do their jobs more efficiently, network with other work-at-home professionals, and gather information where needed.

Associations

American Association of Home
Based Businesses
P.O. Box 10023
Rockville, MD 20849
800-447-9710

American Computer Exchange/AmCoEx
800-786-0717
www.amcoex.com
(matching service for used
computer equipment)

InterExchange AuPair USA
161 Sixth Ave.
New York, NY 10013
800-AUPAIRS

International Association of
Home-Based Businesses
8333 Ralston Rd.
Suite 4
Arvada, CO 80002
800-414-2422

National Association for the Education
of Young Children/NAEYC
1509 16th St. NW
Washington, DC 20036
800-424-2460
www.naeyc.org/naeyc
(accredited preschools)

National Association of Child Care
Professionals
304-A Roanoke St.
Christiansburg, VA 24073
800-537-1118
www.naccp.org

National Association of
Home-Based Businesses
P.O. Box 30220
Baltimore, MD 21270
410-363-3698
www.usahomebusiness.com

National Association of the
Self-Employed/NASE
2121 Precinct Line Rd.
Hurst, TX 76054
800-232-NASE
www.nase.org

Practical Parenting Books
15245 Minnetonka Blvd.
Minnetonka, MN 55345-1510
800-255-3379; FAX: 612-912-0105
www.practicalparenting.com

Service Corps of Retired
Executives/SCORE
409 3rd St. SW, 4th Floor
Washington, DC 20024
800-634-0245
(experienced executives and consulting)

Small Office Home Office/SOHO
2626 East 82nd St., Suite #325
Minneapolis, MN 55425
800-495-SOHO

U.S. Small Business Administration/SBA
409 3rd St. SW
Washington, DC 20416
800-8-ASKSBA
www.sbaonline.sba.gov/

Writer's Digest Book Club
1507 Dana Ave.
Cincinnati, OH 45207
800-289-0963

Newsletters

At Home At Work: The Newsletter
for Parents Who Work from Home
Sharron Kahn, publisher
P.O. Box 487
Mendon, MA 01756
508-634-3989

At-Home Dad
61 Brightwood Ave.
North Andover, MA 01845-1702
athomedad@aol.com

At Work
Berrett-Koehler Publishers, Inc.
155 Montgomery St.
San Francisco, CA 94104-4109

Bottom Line/Personal
Boardroom Reports, Inc.
330 West 42nd St.
New York, NY 10036

Home Business Line
American Home Business Association
397 Post Rd.
Darien, CT 06820

Homeworking Mothers
Mothers' Home Business Network
P.O. Box 423
East Meadow, NY 11554
516-997-7394

Success Working from Home
Jeff Berner
P.O. Box 244, Dept. BK
Dillon Beach, CA 94929

Working Solo newsletter
Portico Press
P.O. Box 190
New Paltz, NY 12561-0190
FAX: 914-255-2116
www.workingsolo.com

Software/videos

Guerrilla Marketing CD-ROM
Houghton Mifflin Interactive
120 Beacon St.
Somerville, MA 02143
800-829-7962; FAX: 800-829-7959

Kiplinger's Guide to Small
  Business Growth Video
c/o Conrad & Associates
1504 Hampton Hills Cir.
McLean, VA 22101
800-553-0504

Microsoft Encarta 97 Encyclopedia
  Deluxe Edition CD-ROM
Microsoft Corporation
One Microsoft Way
Redmond, WA 98052-6399
206-882-8080

1,000+ Stationery Designs
  CD-ROM
Point Pacific Press
P.O. Box 4333
North Hollywood, CA 91617
818-980-2341

The Working Parents Help Book
  (with disk)
Peterson's
P.O. Box 2123
Princeton, NJ 08543-2123
800-338-3282

Web sites for work-at-home professionals

Business

www.smalloffice.com
Home Office/Small Business Computing

http://virtual.office.com/tech/home.html/
Virtual Office resources

www.thelist.com
Pricing on Internet Service Providers

www.hoaa.com
Home Office Association of America

www.hbwm.com
Home-Based Working Moms

www.census.gov
Census Bureau information

www.americanexpress.com/smallbusiness
Small- or home-office information

www.guestfinder.com
Offer your expertise to the media to gain interviews

http://sunsite.unc.edu/personality/keirsey.html
The Keirsey Temperament Sorter

http://nt.excite.com
Excite newstracker, free electronic clipping service

www.newshound.com
Electronic clipping service

http://members.aol.com/lhoberlin/writing.htm
Loriann Hoff Oberlin's *Writing for Money* Web site

Parenting/lifestyle

www.parentsplace.com
www.parentsoup.com
www.practicalparenting.com
www.divorceinfo.com

http://family.com
www.vegsource.com
http://adhere.on.ca/free/

About the author

Loriann Hoff Oberlin contributes to national magazines and news-papers, writing about relationships, parenting, small business concerns, travel, women's issues, and other topics. She has also provided writing, marketing, and public relations support to clients, and regularly teaches workshops and classes.

As the author of *Writing for Money,* Loriann speaks at writer's conferences around the country, encouraging writers to get published and small business owners to market themselves with the written word. She's been a guest on numerous radio and television talk shows and news segments, including the *CNN Morning News.*

In this book, Loriann speaks from experience, raising two young sons and working as a writer, from her home in Pittsburgh, Pa.

Loriann welcomes your comments, with a self-addressed, stamped reply envelope.

Write to: Loriann Hoff Oberlin, P.O. Box 515, Monroeville, PA 15146.

Index

Advertising, 83-85
AIDA technique, 80
Asking for help, 100
Associations, 183-184
Attitude, 179-180
Balance sheet, 31
"Board of Directors," 67
Business
  cards, 33-34
  plans, 30-31
  selecting, 21
Cellular telephones, 61-62
Childcare, 117-132
  au pairs, 120-121
  baby sitters, 125-128
  day-care centers, 121
  family-care settings, 121-122
  illness, 124
  in-home caregivers, 118-120
  out-of-town, 131
  preschools, 128-130
  Rogers, Fred, 122-123
  separation anxiety, 125-126
  special-needs children, 123-124
  taxes, 131
  top 10 list, 127
Children
  activities, 140-152
  advertising, 162
  age-appropriate tasks, 157-158
  allowances, 161
  business etiquette, 162-183
  childproofing your office, 53-54
  chores, 98-100
  clothing, 105-106
  computers, 143-144
  crafts, 146-149
  explaining why you work, 135
  extracurricular activities, 141

  games, 144-145
  Individual Retirement Account
    (IRA), 161
  infants, 137
  money, 161-162
  older, 155-164
  play things, 152
  reading, 141-143
  recipes, 149-151
  running errands with, 140
  special-needs, 123-124
  strengthening family ties, 134-135
  summer, 137-138
  talents, 160
  taxes, 158
  telephone, 146
  television, 142
  travel, 151
  videotapes, 143
  working, 152, 163-164
  younger, 133-153
Collecting, 75-76
Computers, 55-61
  bits per second (bps), 57
  cache, 57
  CD-ROM, 57
  central processing unit (CPU), 56
  children, 143-144
  cleanliness, 60
  clock speed, 56
  crises, 42
  DOS (disk operating system), 56
  external modems, 58-59
  fax/modems, 57, 59
  floppy disk drive, 57
  gigabyte, 57
  graphical user interface (GUI), 56
  hard disk drive, 57
  hard disk, 56

icons, 56
internal modems, 58-59
megabytes (MB), 56
megahertz (MHz), 56
microprocessor, 56
mouse, 56
multimedia systems, 57
printers, 59
RAM (random-access memory), 56
scanners, 58
shopping, 57-59
technical assistance, 60-61
Conservation, 62-63
Crafts, 146-149
  elementary-aged, 147-148
  preschool-aged, 147
Direct mail promotion, 85
Distractions, 95-97
Divorce, 173-174
Downsizing, 19-20
Emergency fund, 35
Etiquette, 162-163
Family support, 21-23
Financial strategies, 35-36
  emergency fund, 35
  pricing, 35-36
Five-year forecast of cash flow, 31
Furniture, 52-53
Goals, 41
Health insurance, 113-114
Hiring, 69-71
  family and friends, 71
  independent contractors, 69-70
  interns, 70
  partnerships, 71
Holidays, 101-103
Housework, 97
Identity, 165-180
  attitude, 179-180
  wardrobe, 177, 179
Independent contractors, 69-70
Individual retirement Account
  (IRA), 161

Infants, 137
Inspiration, 181-182
Insurance, 73-74
  health, 113-114
Internet, 91-93
Interns, 71
Legal assistance, 74
Marriage, 171, 173
Meal-planning, 100-101
Media, the, 82-83
Mistakes, 66
Money, 20-21, 172
  children, 161-162
  collecting, 75-76
  conferences, 108
  raising, 71-73
  records, 73
  saving, 105-114
Money-making ideas, 25-26
  administrative assistance, 25
  arts and crafts, 25
  coffee cart, 26
  computer consulting, 26
  entertainment, 26
  herbs and produce, 25
  home inspections, 25
  home repair, 25
  home-demonstration products, 26
  makeovers, 25
  paralegal, 26
  party planning, 26
  pleasing parents, 26
  tax returns, 25
  transportation, 26
  tutoring, 25
  typing, 25
  Web sites, 26
Moving, 50, 170-171
Myers-Briggs Type Indicator (MBTI), 19
Naming your business, 31-33
National Association for the
  Education of Young Children
  (NAEYC), 129-130

Networking, 68-69
News releases, 81-82
Newsletters, 86-87, 184-185
Nurturing self, 175-176
Occupational Safety and Health
  Administration (OSHA), 16
Office supplies, 109-110
Office-duties day, 42
Organization, 40-42
  computer crises, 42
  files, 41
  goals, 41
  office-duties day, 42
  purging, 49-50
Outside-the-home selling, 54-55
Paper, 110-111
Parents, as bosses, 159
Partnerships, 71
Permits, 37
Pregnancy, 169
Preschools, 128-130
  academic, 129
  cooperative programs, 128
  developmental, 128
  Montessori, 128
  NAEYC, 129-130
  religious, 129
  Waldorf, 128
Pricing, 35-36
Printing, 59, 110-111
Projected income statement, 31
Promotion, 77-94
  advertising, 83-85
  direct mail, 85
  Internet, 91-93
  media, 82-83
  news releases, 81-82
  newsletters, 86-87
  sales calls, 93
  television talk shows, 89-90
  videos and infomercials, 91
  word-of-mouth, 78-79
  writing, 79-82, 88

Put-downs, 167
Recipes, 149-151
Recycling, 62-63
Rogers, Fred, 122-123
Sales calls, 93
Sanity, 178
Scams, 23-24
Selecting a business, 21
Self-contained workspace, 52
Single parents, 130
Size, 66-68
Skills assessment, 19
Spouses, working with, 43
State of mind 44-45
Stationery, 33-34
Taxes, 36, 38-40
  advantages, 158
  advice, 39
  childcare, 131
  home-office scrutiny, 38-39
  receipts, 39-40
Technology, 108-109
Telecommuting, 14-16
Telephone, 146
Television talk shows, 89-90
Time-saving strategies, 103-105
Travel, 139, 107-108, 151, 169-170
Trends, 17-18
Videos and infomercials, 91, 185
Wardrobe, 177-178
Web sites, 26, 185-186
Word-of-mouth promotion, 78-79
Work hours, 34-35
Workaholism, 136-137
Workspace
  childproofing, 53-54
  converting space, 50-53
  furniture, 52-53
  location, 48
  outside the home, 54-55
  self-contained, 52
Writing, 79-82, 88
Zoning, 37